The
Accidental
Systems
Librarian

The
Accidental
Systems
Librarian

Rachel Singer Gordon

 Information Today, Inc.

Medford, New Jersey

First printing, 2003

The Accidental Systems Librarian

Copyright © 2003 by Rachel Singer Gordon

A CIP catalog record for this book is available from the Library of Congress.

Printed and bound in the United States of America.

Publisher: Thomas H. Hogan, Sr.
Editor-in-Chief: John B. Bryans
Managing Editor: Deborah R. Poulson
Copy Editor: Pat Hadley-Miller
Graphics Department Director: M. Heide Dengler
Book Designer: Kara Mia Jalkowski
Cover Designer: Ashlee Caruolo
Indexer: Enid Zafran

Contents

Sidebars

Figures

Foreword

It wasn't that long ago that I first came into contact with Rachel Singer Gordon. I remember how it happened, back in the spring of 2001, when I got an e-mail from her. She had sent a query to me, proposing to write an article for *Computers in Libraries* magazine. For the month she was querying, *CIL*'s theme was "Our Evolving Roles." Rachel's article idea outlined how her own career had evolved.

After library school she took her first entry-level job at a public library outside Chicago. As a younger librarian she was fairly comfortable with PCs, and so she started taking care of some problems, installing some software, etc. As is the case in many jobs, once someone demonstrates an aptitude for certain tasks, others begin to seek her help. A couple years later Rachel found herself in charge of the library computers! Therefore she described herself as an "accidental systems librarian."

I remember thinking what a great title that was. From my experience as the editor of *CIL* (which features articles about library systems) over the years, I had noted that many people were in the same boat. Back when today's middle-aged librarians went to school, the emphasis wasn't on computers. So when they became so prevalent in libraries, the adventurous souls who began toying with them first often became "accidental systems librarians." Although Rachel's situation was slightly different, I knew she'd hit upon a popular concept.

I loved her article query and published "A Course in Accidental Systems Librarianship" that fall (*CIL*, Nov/Dec 01). When I read the first words of that article—"I never wanted to be a computer geek"— I thought, "Amen, sister!" She really struck a chord, and I knew that there were a lot of people who'd appreciate the article. Consequently, I spoke with the editor-in-chief of my company's book division, John Bryans, and he agreed. Thus, this book was born.

I thought I had loved the original article, but I must say I was even more pleasantly surprised with this greatly expanded book version. More than just telling her own tale, Rachel has now covered every aspect of accidental systems librarianship that I can think of. The book starts with the obvious choices of definitions and competencies and moves to technical topics and techniques like installing hardware and software, programming, Web design, dealing with viruses and security issues, and computer troubleshooting. It also covers networking, organization, continuing education, administration, training others, job hunting, and getting the pay you deserve. It even includes samples of tip sheets, problem reports, and forms that you can adapt for your own use. This is definitely a keep-it-forever reference book.

Let me share just one of my favorite quotes. Rachel encourages readers to keep up with listservs, even though everyone is pressed for time: "Managing your time online requires mastery of the grand art of skimming .... Do not feel compelled to read every message that comes through every list. No one will know!" So while she is delivering tips and instructions, she also delivers encouragement, honesty, and humor. These traits come in especially handy in places like Chapter 8, where the author dives in so deep as to explain how to write a tech plan, how to survive a systems migration, and how to manage a staff. Even with the countless diverse responsibilities she discusses, she has a way of making them sound almost easy, and of convincing you that you can handle them.

That's what makes this book great—and so necessary. Rachel has, in essence, laid out a detailed road map to enable others to follow her. For all of you who have stumbled into the role of the systems librarian, this book is the map that will help you survive. Each of you has picked up parts of your job along the way, but since you probably don't have much formal training, you'll be lacking in other areas. This book covers them all, in easy-to-read (and sometimes funny) style.

I think this book fills a niche in the market that nobody has even thought to address before. Sure, there's a plethora of general computer books and plenty of systems books on the IT side. But not many speak to the specific needs of librarians. And none that I know of address the accidental systems administrator, who obviously needs to know more than which wires to put together (or whether to go wireless!). People who don't have strong technical backgrounds need to have things explained a little more carefully, and a little more completely. With all the articles I've read in the literature over the past decade, in my own industry magazine and others, I've come to believe that most library sys-admin folks have arrived in those technical jobs by rather circuitous routes. Sometimes I wonder if there are actually any systems librarians out there who studied for and took that job on purpose!

And so there is this vast group of very smart, well-meaning, hard-working people out there who are slogging through their day-to-day jobs as best they can. Their knowledge often comes from little bits of professional training and a whole lot of self-schooling: reading articles, watching listservs, getting tips from colleagues (or teenagers), going to seminars, etc. But now, at last, these people have one all-encompassing book to guide them. I believe that most systems librarians can use this title to review what they've already picked up and to fill in the gaps in their knowledge. What else could they need?

If you're picking up this book—but never meant to—hang on to it! Written from the experience of someone who's traveled this long road before you, this can be your complete map to success. I guarantee that studying *The Accidental Systems Librarian* will ensure that you feel less lost (and more sane) as you travel your own road.

Kathy Dempsey
kdempsey@infotoday.com

Kathy Dempsey never meant to be a computer geek either. She always loved and worked in libraries; she always knew she wanted to study journalism. So when she landed a job as a journalist in the library field, it was no accident! She's now the proud editor of Computers in Libraries *magazine and* Marketing Library Services *newsletter. She still swears she's not a total geek, even though she reads about libraries and computers all day long.*

Acknowledgments

Like systems librarianship, writing a book is a less than solitary endeavor. I would like to thank the many library professionals who took time from their busy schedules to answer survey questions and participate in interviews, sharing their expertise and experiences with their fellow systems librarians. Thanks also to my publisher, Information Today, Inc., for its dedication to making technology topics accessible and meeting the informational needs of today's librarians. Lastly, thanks to my husband, Todd, who has cheerfully grown accustomed to my spending long hours in front of the computer screen.

About the Web Page
http://www.lisjobs.com/tasl/

As a systems librarian, you know that your job—and the resources you use to carry out your duties successfully—are constantly changing. While this book contains a number of useful Web sites for systems personnel in all types of libraries, the nature of the Web means that pages move, sites change, and new and helpful resources are constantly emerging.

The Web page, available to you as a valued reader of *The Accidental Systems Librarian*, will keep you apprised of these changes, updating links and adding new resources and articles of interest to systems librarians. To access it, go to http://www. lisjobs.com/tasl.

Please feel free to e-mail your comments, changes, or additions to rachel@lisjobs.com.

Introduction

Some of us might wonder just how it is that we became, with neither our knowledge nor our consent, de facto systems geeks.
—Chris Tovell[1]

Many people today who are involved in systems work in libraries fell "accidentally" into their positions, either by assignment, due to a gradual assumption of systems duties, or by luck. In some cases, their careers took an unexpected turn merely because they knew a little bit more about computers (or were younger or had graduated more recently, and were therefore thought to know more about computers!) than their coworkers. In others, these employees felt compelled to take responsibility for computer systems and services because their library's existing technological environment was in some way failing to serve the needs of staff and patrons. Still another group once took "temporary" responsibility for a project or a system and found out too late that such arrangements have a way of becoming permanent. Systems librarians, therefore, come from a variety of backgrounds and enter their positions with both a variety of pre-existing skills and varied levels of technological comfort; most end up learning specific technologies and computer skills on the job.

Many librarians who have assumed responsibility for computer technology in their libraries have had little formal training to prepare them for their new duties. Luckily, traditional library skills have proven to supply a useful background for library systems personnel. Throughout this book, you will see quotes and examples from individuals who have used their backgrounds in librarianship to become effective systems librarians in a variety of institutions and environments. You will also find a number of tools and ideas that will be useful as you prepare yourself for a career in systems librarianship—or begin to settle into your accidental role. Along the way, you will find reassurance: you are not alone, you do not have to be a computer programmer (hacker, MCSE) to serve as a successful systems librarian, and computer skills come and go, while library skills persevere.

In late 2001 through early 2002, 144 systems librarians responded to an online survey on their experiences. (The survey questions are reproduced at the end of the book as Appendix A.) Their responses are quoted throughout the book to help provide insight into the lives of working systems personnel in libraries. Many of the survey respondents emphasize the "accidental" nature of their careers. Typical comments include:

- "I took a night school course in BASIC programming back in 1981. I happened to type DIR at a DOS prompt in front of my supervisor. It was clear to her that I was a computer wizard! And I've been the one-eyed woman in the land of the blind ever since!"

- "As the newest library school graduate at my library I started working with the Internet computers that had just been installed before I came on board. I instituted library Web pages, liaised with computer support, and worked with a team creating one of our first online distance learning classes. Although I had been drawn to cataloging in library school I sort of found my niche in systems."

- "It was the sheerest serendipity, I suppose. When I was working as a library assistant at Yale (in the late 1980s), personal computers were just beginning to become popular in the library world. Although I had no training with PCs (and certainly didn't own one at home ... remember, they were pretty pricy beasts then!), I learned enough on the job that somehow my colleagues came to think of me as possessing 'expertise' (would that it were so!). So I helped support PC users in my department, while still doing my primary job. This carried over into my first professional position—as an acquisitions librarian—and eventually so much of my job became systems-centric that the job was redescribed and I joined the 'Dark Side.'"

- "I have been the youngest and most recent graduate hired into the libraries I have been hired to run. One of the assumptions of those people who hired me was that, due to my age, I was of the technically proficient/wired generation and could do what they did not want to."

- "Completely accidental. I started as a reference and instruction librarian in 1990 with skimpy computer knowledge. But I got involved working on the Gopher and then the Web, and things sort of snowballed from there. I'm almost entirely self-taught."

- "My employers just tend to put me in these kinds of jobs. I never had any intention of doing this sort of thing, but apparently there is a great need for it and I apparently have an aptitude for it. I was put on this path pretty much by chance."

- "… because we needed to select an automation system, the director added to my duties the task of heading up the selection committee and then installing the system. It was to be temporary. That needs to be underlined, because years later, I was still doing the job. Everyone thought at the time that the system would run itself. That is, we'd install it, get everyone trained, and the only thing that would need doing is running overdue notices. Right."

- "If I had been offered this training in library school, I probably would not have chosen to pursue it. I'm not really a geek—I'm an English major, for god's sake!"

The accidental nature of much systems work in libraries is exacerbated by the propensity of librarians to want to solve problems. Many of us got started working with library technology merely because our library happened to have a technological issue (or issues) needing a solution, and we had the skills (or willingness) to work to find the answer. And, one truism of library work is this: if you do something once, it becomes yours forever.

Since so many of us are accidental systems personnel, and since systems librarianship is a relatively newer field, compared to traditional departments such as cataloging and reference, there has been insufficient practical material written that is intended to help give systems librarians the skills they need to succeed—especially material that is intended to show them how to use their library background to gain or feign such skills. This may seem surprising to librarians who feel overwhelmed with an onslaught of Internet articles, but most of these focus on search techniques or philosophical issues rather than hands-on systems advice. While a number of titles provide a basic introduction to technology for library managers, or for general staff working with technology in their day-to-day tasks, the literature addressing those who have made systems work their primary responsibility is fragmented. Further, there has been little specific attention given (aside from the creation of basic "computer competencies" at a number of individual libraries) to mapping out how nonsystems staff, whose responsibilities nevertheless require working with computer technology, can call on their library background to develop the ability to use such technology effectively.

Throughout this book, you will find advice and information to help you manage and interact with computer technology in your institution, whatever your level of systems responsibility. Chapters 1 and 2 provide a background in systems librarianship, outlining the skills that may be needed and attempting to define the specialty. Chapters 3–4 show how traditional library skills such as the organization of knowledge and research techniques form the foundation of a successful career in systems. Chapters 6–7 discuss learning and teaching, focusing on instruction techniques for teaching others, and independent study skills for extending your own knowledge. Chapter 8 addresses more advanced topics, describing how library systems personnel can tackle managing large projects and managing systems staff. Chapter 9 emphasizes the real-world aspect of working with library systems and provides information on finding a job in the field (or related fields) and dealing with its attendant stresses. The conclusion and appendices round out your whirlwind course of instruction, providing resources for further reading and study. Although tips, suggestions, and descriptions of library technology are included throughout, this is not a "how-to" guide outlining every aspect of managing public-access computers or integrated library systems. Instead, this course of study shows you how to use and extend your library skills to give yourself the background you need to succeed.

Throughout the book, the terms systems librarian, automation librarian, technology librarian, and computer services librarian will be used interchangeably, reflecting the diversity of position titles in today's libraries.

I have myself worked as an accidental systems librarian, serving as a one-person department for several years in a smaller public library. Many of the recommendations in this book are based on my own experiences, as well as on conversations with colleagues in a variety of library environments. I hope that you find systems librarianship as exciting and dynamic a field as I have, and that these suggestions, resources, and stories prove helpful in your career. Please feel free to contact me with your comments and reactions.

Rachel Singer Gordon
rachel@lisjobs.com

Works Cited

1. Tovell, Chris. "Whippersnappers vs. the Old Guard? Making E-Resources Training a Collaborative Experience." *Info Career Trends*, September 2001. 4 Jan. 2002 (http://www.lisjobs.com/newsletter/archives/sept01ctovell.htm).

Chapter 1

Systems Librarianship 101: Defining Systems Librarianship

People have different expectations today than they did under the homogeneous stereotypes imposed by broadcast media. We resent being labeled and categorized.

—Christopher Locke[1]

Standardizing on an appropriate definition for systems librarianship as a specialty bears an unfortunate resemblance to attempting to define what constitutes obscenity. Most people just "know it when they see it," yet a useful and concise description remains elusive. This is due partially to the newness of the field as compared to traditional subfields of librarianship and partially to the difficulty many people encounter in fitting the wide variety of tasks systems librarians engage in into one coherent schema. Depending on the size, type, funding, needs, and philosophy of their institutions, systems librarians may have duties as diverse as:

- Computer hardware selection, installation, and troubleshooting

- Software selection, installation, and support

- Local and/or wide area network administration and security responsibilities

- Internet support, including router, proxy server, and firewall configuration

- Security and stability of the public computing environment

- Web page design and maintenance

- General help desk functions

- Database vendor liaison

- Electronic resource selection and implementation

- Original script programming

- Digitizing, archiving, and cataloging document, audio, and video collections

- Intranet support and design

- Staff and patron technology training

- Integrated Library System (ILS) maintenance and automation migration, upgrades, and training

- Database development and programming

- Project management

- Creating technical documentation

- Creating RFPs and required system specifications for vendors

Systems librarians may be responsible for any or all of these functions, for additional functions, or for an entirely different (or as yet unimagined!) set of duties. In addition to the specific technological tasks in the above list, they may also have budgetary and management accountability, as well as responsibility for more traditional library functions such as reference and cataloging.

To add to the confusion, systems librarians may or may not have earned an MLS. Systems-related tasks may be a part of their job or comprise their full set of responsibilities. Librarians may work as part of an information technology (IT) department, manage a systems department, serve as a liaison to such a department, assume half-time systems duties, or exist as a department of one (or solo librarian), their library's sole source of automation support. Their library may be part of a larger system or institution that assumes part of the burden of supporting technology in the library, or it may be a stand-alone library with no nonvendor outside source of technical support. Each systems librarian position, therefore, comes with a unique blend of responsibilities.

Job titles of those who work with computer technology in libraries also vary tremendously from library to library. A random sampling of titles from the systems librarian survey results in labels as diverse as:

- Network Services Librarian

- Head of Reference/Systems Coordinator

- Systems Librarian

- Technology Coordinator

- Manager, Systems

- Principal Librarian for Automation and Technical Services

- Electronic Information Systems Librarian

- Information Technology Librarian

- Automation Librarian

- Support Team Leader

- Assistant Library Director/Computer Systems Manager

There are countless other variations on the theme. Some librarians with automation responsibilities, however, especially solo librarians or those in smaller institutions, will have no terms in their title indicating they have taken on such responsibilities.

As librarians, we do tend to feel a certain level of discomfort with that which cannot easily be categorized. This variety in background, title, and tasks, however, is confusing only if we allow ourselves to be blinded by the technological aspect. More traditional library positions also vary tremendously in scope and duties by type of library. No one, however, seriously suggests that a reference librarian in a small, largely nonautomated, rural library; one in a largely electronic news library; and one in a size-able research institution are not each clearly serving as reference staff—even though the types of questions they receive, the specific tools they use, and their daily tasks may look quite different. What matters is that librarians are using their reference background to assist library patrons in answering questions and researching topics of interest.

Note also that a number of the job titles in the previous list reflect systems librarians' dual roles in systems and reference or in systems and technical services. Another difficulty in defining systems librarianship occurs because, historically, librarians have taken on systems duties in addition to their existing responsibilities, rather than stepping immediately into a full-fledged systems role. This assumption of technological duties often happens gradually, so that systems work becomes identified in that institution as belonging under an existing department rather than as a specialty in its own right. Further, technology itself becomes so intertwined with all aspects of library operations that it seems difficult to define systems librarianship as a specific subfield; systems librarians have a hand in the running of each department. As library technology becomes more complex and demanding, however, many librarians who previously held one of these dual roles find the balance of their duties shifting toward systems work. Given this inevitable shift, it may be useful, again, to think of systems responsibilities in the same way we think of reference or technical services responsibilities. Even in smaller institutions where one person tends to fill dual (or multiple) roles, departments and responsibilities are clearly identifiable as belonging to specific subfields of librarianship.

Another difficulty in definition stems from the tendency to define systems work as outside the purview of librarianship and as falling in the realm of "the IT department" or as the responsibility of "computer technicians." This view is shortsighted, reflecting nostalgia for a precomputerized era, a false separation of computer and other technologies, and a lack of understanding that librarians have been involved with the development of technologies that met library needs from the very inception of such tools. (The development of the MARC standard is a preeminent example of such involvement. A fascinating photo history of "computing and libraries," compiled by Buffalo professor Chris Brown-Syed, is available at http://valinor.ca/computing.) We should also not forget libraries' involvement with and use of technologies from the typewriter to microfilm, each of which was used and supported in—and served to transform—our institutions long before the computer age.

We cannot abandon such an integral aspect of library operations to nonlibrarians, since the ways in which we implement and support technology in our libraries affect all of our departments and services. Supporting computer technology does not make you a technician, it makes you a librarian with systems responsibilities. Roy Tennant sums it up best: "Today, in this digital world, professional work *is* technical."[2] Librarianship and systems responsibilities go hand-in-hand, and their skill sets are both complementary and required for any computer services librarian.

Eric Lease Morgan, head of digital access and information architecture at University Libraries of Notre Dame, notes: "I consider myself to be a librarian first and a computer user second. My professional goal is to discover new ways to use computers to improve library and knowledge services. There in [sic] lies the essence of systems librarianship. *Systems librarianship is the art and science of combining the principles of librarianship with the abilities of computing technology* [emphasis in original]."[3] Because of this, non-MLS systems personnel can find they have as much learning to do on the library side as librarians who assume systems duties have to do on the technology side. The successful systems librarian blends both outlooks and skill sets in finding the appropriate balance for her institution.

Library Skills and Communication

A library background is crucial to doing effective systems work in libraries. Although some larger institutions may make the decision to staff their official systems departments entirely with computer science personnel that lack either MLS degrees or library work experience, and some smaller institutions may try to get by with part-time technical help from computer science students, this tends to lead to gaps in communication and outlook between IT and the rest of the institution. MLS systems librarians working in institutions with separate IT departments often find themselves acting to bridge these gaps, which highlights the necessity of being able to communicate equally well with technical staff, librarians, the library administration, and patrons. One of the most important roles of any systems librarian in a larger institution is that of liaison between librarians and the IT department, and, in smaller institutions, that of liaison between patrons, librarians, and the technology itself. Communication and people skills are paramount for any technology librarian, as is the ability to view systems issues from both a library and an IT perspective.

Many survey respondents emphasize the importance of bridging such communication gaps. Michelle Mach, Web librarian at Colorado State University Libraries, describes her role as liaison as follows: "Our systems department does not have any librarians, so as a librarian with a technical job I find that I use my librarian mindset every day to bridge the gap between the other librarians and the systems department. Communication is always an issue.

Seemingly minor decisions like changing the Web browser on the public terminals from Netscape to IE have caused a near uproar simply because the decisions were made by the systems department without first discussing it with the reference staff." OHSU Library Systems and Cataloging Head Janet Crum concurs: "Much of my job consists of being a liaison among library staff, vendors, and our campus IT department. To perform that role effectively, I must understand library needs and operations thoroughly and be able to explain them, especially to IT staff. In many cases I am a translator, translating IT-speak to librarians and library-speak to IT staff. Without a thorough grounding in the principles and practice of librarianship, I could not perform this function effectively."

As you advance in your career, and the more you learn on both the library and the technical sides, the more effectively you will be able to communicate with all these constituencies. Your library background will give you credibility with staff and patrons, while your technology knowledge provides an entrée into the world of IT. As Julie Bozell remarks in an online interview: "Once I picked up some lingo, I found MIS stopped talking so down to me and more things seem[ed] to get fixed, or I now actually found I had more knowledge to just fix things on my own."[4] Julie describes the importance of gaining some familiarity with technology in order to gain credibility and work effectively with an IT staff. Your familiarity will also help you see things from the IT perspective and understand the reasoning behind their actions.

It is precisely because technology is interwoven throughout library operations that systems librarians are essential in ensuring that technology always serves the needs of the institution. If a library lacks systems support or lacks librarians able to interface with its IT department, technology may either fail to meet institutional needs, or it will just plain fail. One of the reasons that library skills are so useful in managing library technology is that one of the systems librarians' main responsibilities lies in using their background in the principles of librarianship to communicate with all library constituents and determine how technology can be used most effectively. This includes communication to bridge the gap between techies and nontechies; communication with the library's users to ensure that their needs are being met by the current technological environment; communication with library staff and patrons when training, providing technical support, or creating documentation; communication with the library's administration to ensure they understand the importance of funding technology and training; and communication with software and hardware vendors to convey the library's unique needs and existing technological environment.

Despite the popular image of librarians as asocial individuals locked away in rooms full of dusty books, we have always recognized the importance of interacting with others. This is doubly necessary in a systems environment, where miscommunication is all too easy. As Eric Lease Morgan writes in his survey response: "Systems work is people work, not necessarily computer work. Eighty percent (80%) of any problem is related to working with people (getting their input, writing documentation, testing, usability, etc.) and only 20% is actually hacking at code."

While systems librarians coming from a library background must work to extend their technology skills and vocabulary in order to communicate effectively with IT departments and vendors, systems personnel in libraries who come from an IT background and find themselves in this role of liaison encounter the opposite difficulty. They have the technology skills but may lack the background to use them effectively in a library environment or to communicate effectively with library staff and users. IT personnel tend to be heavy on jargon and may emphasize library systems over the people who use them. IT people who find themselves in library roles need to acquaint themselves with the unique requirements of libraries and with the user-centered foundations of the profession. One survey respondent succinctly notes: "I've noticed that systems people without a library background are sometimes not aware there are real people using our products." IT people (and this also extends to systems librarians) must also realize the importance of keeping the lines of communication open when there is a problem with computing equipment or services. While nontechnical library staff will understandably be frustrated when a service or machine is "down," they will be more understanding if they are kept informed as to the progress of the situation's potential resolution.

Realize also that there is no one right way to communicate with others in your institution. One of your goals, for example, will be to communicate to nonsystems staff how they can use technology effectively in their day-to-day activities. There are a number of ways to do this, ranging from informal one-on-one conversations ("Did you know …") to formal training classes to providing printed and online documentation. You might create a regular newsletter of computer tips that you can photocopy and distribute, send via e-mail, or post on your intranet—whichever will reach your colleagues most effectively. You can create tip sheets and brochures describing various aspects of the library's computer technology that public services staff can hand out to patrons and refer to when assisting library visitors. You can archive tip sheets in a subject-divided binder at public services desks so that staff can quickly find half-remembered information. You can create a "what's new in computers" PowerPoint slide show that staff can run on their own PCs or that runs on an old PC placed in the corner of the staff room. You can send out tips and reminders explaining how to accomplish infrequent tasks, since people are likely to forget if they do not use a feature often.

Try to think of creative ways of getting people to use technology more effectively and efficiently in your own environment. When creating these resources, however, keep your audience in mind. Do not inflict excessive jargon on nontechnical library staff, and do not overload them with extraneous information. Keep tips and instructions straightforward, to the point, and useful. Your job is to enable staff to use technology to do their jobs more effectively.

If your library is large or tends to have heavy turnover, consider creating a computer procedures manual for public services staff that explains common uses of technology in the library. You can use this while training new staff members, and newer individuals can use this as a resource to turn to when they are alone at the desk and no systems support is available. The manual should outline basics such as the process for turning on and logging in machines each morning, lists of the software that is available on the public workstations, basic troubleshooting steps for common problems, and so on. Consider creating equivalent manuals for other departments as your institution's needs dictate; work with department heads to see what specific processes their staff might need to have outlined for them.

Lastly, understand the necessity of effective communication with your library's administration. You will need to help administrators understand the importance of funding technology projects, staffing technology departments, and allotting sufficient time and resources to your efforts. If your administration is less technologically savvy, they may have difficulty seeing why costly time, funding, and personnel should be allocated to technology when other departments and projects are also clamoring for funding and attention. You will need to work with your administration on grants, technology plans, and large-scale projects, which requires you to be able to outline the benefits of your proposals and to describe ideas in nontechnical language. (See more on this in Chapter 8.) You will also need to help your administration understand that technology and related expenses such as staffing and training are necessarily ongoing. Too often, institutions have funded technology as a one-time allocation on an adhoc, as-needed basis and will need convincing of the necessity of consistent funding.

Sample "Tips and Tricks" Computer Newsletter
Franklin Park Public Library (March 2001)

Find It Fast

When searching for information on the Internet, use the "Find in Page" feature to help you jump to just the right place in a long document. When a Web page is up on the screen, hit Ctrl-F to bring up the "find" window. Type in the word or phrase you are looking for, hit <ENTER>, and it will bring you to that spot on the page.

Web Site Highlight

What's new on our Web site this month? Find:

- Local History "search the site" quiz. Check it out to find out more about local history information on our site and to practice searching.

- Links to printable federal and state tax forms from the front page of our site.

Remember, you can get to the Web site by clicking on the top of the staff Web page or by going to: http://www.franklinparklibrary.org

Power Outage?

If the power goes out, there are a couple of things we need to do to ensure that the computers come back up OK.

1) If the power stays out for more than a couple of minutes, shut all of the computers down normally—just as you would at night—and turn them off.

2) If the power is out for more than about 10 minutes, when the power comes back on, you will need to turn the server back on before any of the computers can log back into the network.

3) The server is in Tech Services, in the back corner by the window where all the wires are. It is the giant PC on the bottom shelf. Make sure it is off (check to see if there is a light on the front). If it is off, press the power button and give it about 3 minutes to boot back up. Then login the other computers as you would normally.

4) The lasers at Circ will need to be reset. Before turning on the circ PCs, unplug both lasers and plug them back in. They are plugged into the power strips on the floor, and are large plugs that say "Intermec."

Yes, You Are a Systems Librarian!

Any library, no matter how small, needs to find someone willing and able to take responsibility for its computer technology. As soon as one PC goes on a desk, somebody is needed to support that technology—whether or not that library has a formal IT department, and whether or not anyone is formally prepared to assume that role. If you have found yourself in one of these accidental roles, and your job title and compensation have not changed to match your new duties, do not hesitate to bring up the topic with your library's administration. (See more on negotiating promotions in Chapter 9.) Take the initiative to try and clarify the boundaries of your own position; offer to help draft a new job description that reflects your systems as well as your nonsystems responsibilities. Most administrations recognize the importance of smoothly running technology in today's library and will be willing to work with you on these points.

Although some librarians' technological skills obviously become more specialized to fit their institutions' needs, a basic facility with technology is now needed by all librarians. The more you know, the more effectively you can use technology to serve your staff and patrons' needs, instead of the other way around. While you may not have thought to define yourself as a systems librarian, if you have any responsibilities for supporting and implementing technology, you have responsibilities that fall under the cloak of systems librarianship—in the same way that a children's librarian who works at the adult reference desk one day a week can be said to have reference responsibilities. This makes us all, in some sense, systems librarians. As Mayo and Nelson note: "Everyone working in libraries today is part of the technological revolution whether they want to be or not."[5]

It therefore behooves you to take the time to learn the skills to serve effectively in your position. The more you learn to use your library background to help you discharge your systems responsibilities, the more effectively you can carry out this portion of your job. As Eileen Lutzow, systems and electronic resources librarian at Charleston Southern University, writes in her response to the survey: "Systems administration puts you into every area of the library, so knowing something about each area is useful … I think librarians can pick up the 'techie' details they need faster than 'techies' can pick up the library knowledge they need, though there are exceptions to either scenario."

Systems librarians with full-time responsibilities for technology in their libraries will, of course, devote more of their time and education to their specialty. But realizing that we all share similar responsibilities helps bridge the perceived gap between systems librarianship and other subfields of the profession as well as encourages nonsystems librarians to take responsibility for familiarizing themselves with technology. All librarians today require some technological literacy to carry out their duties effectively. Nonsystems staff needs to be able to use computer technology effectively and to assist patrons in using such technology. They need to be able to do minor troubleshooting when systems staff is not available, and public services personnel are also fielding more technical questions from their patrons, who expect librarians to be knowledgeable about technological issues. Eric Lease Morgan says it best when asking: "In today's world, why would anybody trust a librarian, whose profession is about information and knowledge, who hadn't mastered a computer?"[6] You may have some difficulty convincing your fellow staff members of this truth, but librarians today must come to realize that computers are integral to both library functions and their own jobs.

Writing in *American Libraries,* Joyce Latham points out that: "True functional literacy in a library organization begins when front-line staff start to accept responsibility for how their technical installations function and explore just how much they can do with them. Another important moment in the development of institutional literacy occurs when administrators begin to explore ways to crisscross these service areas, involving librarians in technical problem solving and technical staff in public program design. Creating avenues for communication and partnership between these two groups is key to developing the inherent potential of technology."[7] Literacy today includes technological literacy, and we librarians cannot pass such literacy on to our patrons if we do not all first obtain basic technological skills of our own.

Another part of your responsibility as a systems librarian, therefore, will be to help transfer appropriate technological skills and a comfort with technology to other library staff—and to your administration. Find more on training both staff and patrons in Chapter 6, but for now realize the importance of communication skills in inculcating technological literacy and the importance of having technologically literate staff. This is as true in the smallest public library as it is in the largest research institution.

Establishing Competencies

If you are in a larger institution with staff from varying backgrounds and with varying levels of computer competence, it will be useful to establish basic technological competencies for all staff. Official computer services staff will, of course, be expected to attain a higher degree of competency with library computer systems than will nonsystems personnel, but you can identify and require the necessary minimum requirements for all staff for the smooth use and running of technology in your library. Competencies define the basic computer skills expected of library staff, and must therefore be observable, measurable, and improvable. Establishing computer competencies for all recognizes that technology is integral in all departments, allows staff to use technology effectively to meet institutional needs, and allows systems librarians to concentrate their efforts on more complex issues, rather than continually helping other staff members with the basics.

Your library's technology competencies should reflect the specific skills that are necessary for staff to carry out their daily duties effectively. To determine individuals' existing levels of competency with your institution's systems and software, it will be useful to create a checklist of desired skills and then to allow staff members to evaluate their own levels of comfort with completing those skills. Emphasize that this is not a test, and that no one's job performance will be graded on these sheets. The goal is for complete honesty so that you can evaluate the areas in which you need to shore up staff skills and provide targeted training, cheat sheets, and other resources to help people use technology to do their jobs.

Staff Competencies

Recognize that nearly every library position, whether professional or paraprofessional, now requires the use of a computer. For the sake of library productivity and staff sanity, employees need to acquire the skills to use the computer in their daily work. When developing your competencies, therefore, target them to the tasks that will be useful to staff in their day-to-day activities. In a larger institution, it will be useful to create competencies for each job description or classification; in a smaller library, competencies by department may suffice. For an example of thorough, albeit dated, staff technology competencies by job description, see the Oakland Public Library's at http://www.oaklandlibrary.org/techcomp.htm. The New Jersey Library Association has posted a more general set of the technical competencies recommended for all New Jersey librarians at www.njla.org/statements/techcompetencies.html. These competencies include items such as "knows internet terminology, such as URL, search engine, home page, link, web site, tool bar, status bar, scroll bar," and "accesses library email programs to compose, send and reply to email." Looking at these more general competencies may be useful as a starting point for creating your own set; customize as necessary for your institution's computing environment. One last useful example is the Rochester Regional Library Council's set of core competencies, which includes a number of resources for self-study and checklists for self-testing. See http://www.rrlc.org/competencies/techcomp.html.

If your library's environment includes a number of different software packages, electronic databases, and hardware configurations, you might consider breaking these core competencies down by subject area. Create a competency checklist (or a "basic" and "advanced" checklist) for Windows usage, each Microsoft Office program, one for Internet usage, one for your e-mail software, one for basic hardware knowledge, and so on. Be sure to update these lists whenever the library changes software packages or upgrades; keep them current so that they are always a usable tool.

Sample Questions for an Internet Explorer Competency Self-Assessment Test

Please rate your comfort with completing the following tasks on a scale of 1 to 3, with 3 being "very comfortable" and 1 being "not at all comfortable."

I am able to type an Internet address into the address bar to visit a particular Web page.
  1   2   3

I am able to use "Print Preview" to select certain pages of a document for printing.
  1   2   3

I can use the "Find" function to locate a word or phrase within a particular Web page.
  1   2   3

I can copy and paste a Web address from my e-mail or other application into Internet Explorer.

   1   2   3

I know how to use toolbar buttons to move "back," "forward," and "home."

   1   2   3

I know how to clear the history in Internet Explorer.

   1   2   3

After staff members have been tested (or have self-tested) on these technological basics, you will wish to use the results to determine the need for training to bring all staff up to appropriate levels of technical knowledge. (See more on creating and implementing a staff training program in Chapter 6.) Formal training can be supplemented with online tutorials, "cheat sheets," and other self-study materials for staff. Once staff members have completed training, have them retest themselves on your competency checklists.

Systems Competencies

After mastering the basic competencies required of all staff, systems personnel should go on to acquire the additional competencies necessary for the smooth running of library technology. While basic staff competencies will tend to be similar for personnel in most libraries (who mainly utilize Microsoft Windows, standard browser software, integrated library system [ILS] modules, Microsoft Office software, and so on), the specific competencies required of systems personnel will look radically different in different institutions. These competencies need to match the duties assumed by each systems librarian and the software and hardware environment in their institutions.

The Federal Library and Information Center Committee of the Library of Congress has posted a general list of "Knowledge, Skills, and Abilities" for systems librarians at http://www.loc.gov/flicc/wg/ksa-sys.html. Note that these are not all strictly "technical" skills, and that this is a list intended for use in drafting job ads for systems personnel. Still, this gives you a useful starting point for drafting systems competencies for your institution, adapting and adding more specific skills as necessary. Each of these general areas can be broken down into specific tasks or competencies and made more specific in terms of the technology used in your institution.

If you do have a systems staff, consider creating competencies for each position within your department that will reflect that individual's specific duties. This will help you to see if the skills of current staff members need upgrading and to evaluate new hires for specific skills needed. It will also enable you to balance workload and duties among staff according to their areas of expertise. If you do not have a staff, you may be in the awkward position of creating competencies for yourself—which is especially difficult if you are just starting or working your way into a systems position and do not necessarily know what you need to know. To create competencies in this situation, it will be useful to start by making an inventory of the software and hardware used in the library. Evaluate what you are responsible for supporting, and begin to think about how you would like to improve the library's technological environment in the future. This will give you a base point for creating competencies for yourself and finding out what you may need to learn.

Systems Librarians as Change Agents

Beyond the specific responsibilities that systems librarians hold in common for the smooth running of library technology, they hold similar personal responsibilities for maintaining a flexible outlook and fostering the capacity to both accept and facilitate technological change within their institutions. While the previous sections have focused on defining systems librarianship in terms of common skills and tasks, a commonality of outlook is equally important. Just as librarians as a group share a common foundation of principles and philosophy, so too do systems librarians.

In the not-too-recent past, librarianship was seen as an extremely stable profession. We all had a fairly clear picture in our minds of what a library was supposed to look like (thanks to Carnegie), what it contained (books), and what a librarian's job entailed (selecting, looking up information in, and maintaining the order of those books). From such mind pictures stereotypes are made, and of course libraries of all types and sizes, and librarians of all descriptions, have always flourished. Yet historically, many have been drawn to this profession largely because of its perceived stability and from a love for the permanence of the written word and the books housed in our institutions.

The principles of our profession have not changed, but the containers of information and the methods we use to access such information have. What is most distressing to many is the rapidity of such change; a given organization may have moved from providing print-only collections to adding one stand-alone CD-ROM station to setting up a bank of Internet terminals providing access to a number of subscription databases—all within a few short years. As systems librarians, however, we can afford neither to be blinded by appearances nor stunned by change. We must concentrate on the way we can best facilitate access to all parts of our collection today. We must also be open to new technologies and new methods of information storage and retrieval tomorrow and should, in fact, welcome and work to develop such technologies if they offer advantages to the users of our library's resources. This is not to say that any technological change is automatically desirable merely because it is possible, but that a primary goal is to facilitate those changes that help our institution carry out its mission. A secondary role is to help our fellow librarians adapt to these inevitable changes.

We should always view the prospect of technological change as librarians first and technologists second. IT people may wish to implement a technology because it is new, cool, and different, but, as librarians, we understand that technology serves the institution rather than vice versa. While as systems people we should be comfortable with and appreciate the power of computing technology, as librarians we should appreciate that technology is merely a tool. As Mark Stover explains: "As librarians gain more power and responsibilities in the arena of information technology, we must not lose sight of our core values as a profession. We have a special imperative to shape the new age of computing with the traditions and values of those who came before us in the information professions."[8] As change agents, we again find ourselves in the role of liaison between technological possibility and institutional goals.

Works Cited

1. Locke, Christopher. "Preface to the Paperback Edition." Rick Levine, et al. *The Cluetrain Manifesto: The End of Business as Usual.* Cambridge: Perseus Publishing, 2000, 2001: ix.

2. Tennant, Roy. "Honoring Technical Staff." *Library Journal*, May 15, 2001. 4 May 2002 (http://libraryjournal.reviewsnews.com/index.asp?layout=articleArchive&articleId=CA75217).

3. Morgan, Eric Lease. "On Being A Systems Librarian." April 30, 1996, rev. January 1, 2001. 30 January, 2002 (http://www.infomotions.com/musings/systems-librarianship.shtml).

4. Schwartz, Mark. "Librarians and Technology: An Interview with Julie Bozzell." February 15, 2002. 1 May, 2002 (http://www.llrx.com/features/bozzell.htm).

5. Mayo, Diane, and Sandra Nelson. *Wired for the Future: Developing Your Library Technology Plan.* Chicago: ALA Editions, 1999: 49.

6. Morgan, Eric Lease. "Computer Literacy for Librarians." *Computers in Libraries*, Jan. 1998: 39.

7. Latham, Joyce. "The World Online: IT Skills for the Practical Professional." *American Libraries*, March 2000: 41.

8. Stover, Mark. *Leading the Wired Organization: The Information Professional's Guide to Managing Technological Change.* New York: Neal-Schuman, 1999: 331.

Chapter 2

Systems Librarianship 102: Technical Areas You May Need to Master

*Scratch an expert and you'll often find someone
who's muddling through—just at a higher level.*
—Steve Krug[1]

The body of knowledge required to be a successful systems librarian is a constantly shifting target. The rapid pace of technological change, coupled with the wide range of library environments and technologies, ensures that you will have something, and usually many things, to learn when taking on any computer-related position. What is important to remember is that technical skills can be acquired; try not to let an explicit list of technical requirements scare you out of applying for a position or taking on a project. You can learn to work with any program, OS, automation system, or hardware configuration as needed. (This is why crash courses exist! See more on extending your technological skills in Chapter 7.) Specific technical skills are secondary; what matters most to your success as a systems librarian are your openness to learning, your capacity to both embrace and facilitate change, and your foundation in the principles of librarianship.

Lists of what all computer services librarians "need to know" are inherently suspect. What these lists generally embody is either a rundown of the competencies for working in a particular institution or the ideals, background, and philosophy of a particular systems manager. While nonsystems librarians may have difficulty understanding that systems librarianship is still a field of librarianship, systems people sometimes get caught up in an idealized view of what work with technology in libraries should be. Especially among more technically advanced systems personnel in larger libraries, there is a certain tendency to assume that all systems librarians should possess the same competencies and to spend time arguing over what does or does not constitute true systems librarianship. This is unnecessarily divisive and does little to boost the confidence of many accidental technology librarians who lack expertise in one of these "true" systems areas but are nonetheless quite effective in their positions.

What you as a systems librarian truly need to know (or to learn) is determined by factors such as the technological environment in your library, the goals of your institution, the needs of your staff and patrons, and the support you receive from your larger institution or library system/consortium. Do not waste time or energy worrying about what you should or could know, or what other systems librarians in other institutions might know. (You have enough other issues to concern yourself with.) Instead, learn what you need to know for your particular set of circumstances. In essence, try to acquire the knowledge necessary for the effective support of technology in your library, and to extend that knowledge with the goal of improving patron and staff interactions with technology. Always remain open to acquiring new knowledge and learning about new technologies. This openness and willingness to learn will also stand you in good stead if you later choose to seek a systems position in another library, whose environment likely differs from yours.

There are, however, a number of similar tasks shared by systems librarians in different institutions. Technology in libraries can take only so many forms, so the following sections will take you on a whirlwind tour of technology librarians' typical broad areas of expertise. Your institutional environment may require familiarity with one, none, or all of these areas, or with more specific technologies and methods not covered here. Note that this list is less than comprehensive; it is included to give you an idea of the technologies systems librarians may need to familiarize themselves with and to provide suggestions on setting up systems in an effective way. While library technology encompasses items from photocopiers to microfilm, we are here talking just about computer technology in libraries. Be forewarned, however; administrators and staff members sometimes have a tendency to assume that computer expertise translates into a general familiarity with all machines. Be prepared to fend off requests to take on duties such as repairing photocopiers and poking into the innards of recalcitrant cash registers.

Do not panic if you are less than an expert in one or more of these topics. Descriptions are meant for background purposes only, as an overview of current common technologies needing systems librarian support. Reading these sections will not endow you with instant expertise but will provide you with a foundation and with ideas for learning on your own. A number of resources are listed in each section; use these as a starting point for further reading. The preponderance of these resources pertain either to newer technologies with which you may be less likely to be familiar or to heavily used technologies with an existing broad base of support. Realize also that this list would have looked very different 10 years ago, and it will likely be transformed again in the next 10—or fewer. Note that the evolutionary nature of systems librarianship and the limited funding available for upgrading technology in many libraries also means that you may be responsible for simultaneously supporting multiple types or generations of technology: both dumb terminals and PCs, or Macs and PCs, or CD-ROMs and online resources, for example.

Microsoft Software

Microsoft's desktop dominance extends to libraries as well as to the business world. Many libraries' computing environments contain a mix of Windows-based operating systems, from Windows 95 to 98 to NT to 2000 to XP. If at all possible, try to standardize your institution's client machines on a particular version of an operating system, which will simplify troubleshooting and provide a more stable and consistent environment for staff and users. Resist the urge to upgrade as soon as a new version of a Microsoft operating system appears, as patches and service packs are surely soon to follow. Since stability is so important in a library environment, older technologies may suffice for quite some time.

Beyond their Windows-based client machines, a number of libraries maintain a Windows NT/2000 server, or servers, as the center of their local area network. (Read more on networking later in this chapter.) Microsoft's tendency to heavily discount client access licenses and software used in educational (including academic and public library) environments is one factor in ensuring that the company's dominance in the library server market is likely to continue. Windows NT and 2000 networks, furthermore, are comparatively easy to set up and maintain, making Windows-based servers a logical choice for libraries whose network administrators are also accidental systems librarians.

Microsoft's overall dominance, however, also makes it an attractive target for crackers, virus creators, and other malicious individuals. If you use a Windows-based server in your network, make it a priority to keep that server up-to-date with the latest security patches, service packs, and recommendations. A number of libraries have experienced heavy damage to their systems through hacker attacks (generally by either disgruntled patrons or former staff members—it should go without saying that ex-staff members' access should be removed the day they depart your institution). Others have fallen prey to opportunistic worms such as Nimda, which, for example, shut down such large systems as Fairfax County and Fort Wayne's Community school district in September 2001. At a minimum, faithfully update your antivirus software definitions, keep your server(s) behind a firewall, and patch your server(s) on a timely basis in order to reduce the likelihood of this occurring in your institution. You may wish to subscribe to a product such as kbAlertz (http://www.kbalertz.com), which will regularly e-mail updates of knowledge base additions on the products you choose. Also, familiarize yourself with Microsoft's online security portal (http://www.microsoft.com/security [see Figure 2.1]) and be sure to visit often or sign up for their e-mail notification service on security issues. While there, download the Microsoft Baseline Security Analyzer, which allows you to scan your systems for known vulnerabilities. Automated patch tools are worth investigating as well, although users have reported mixed experiences with these.

Figure 2.1   Microsoft Security Portal

Your institution also likely makes use of the Microsoft Office software suite. Microsoft Office software is one area in which you may receive some assistance from other library staff members in answering questions and teaching other users. Its longevity as the predominant office suite has resulted in a large base of "power users" familiar with the ins and outs and tips and tricks of dealing with the software. Note, however, that documents created with newer versions of Office software are not necessarily compatible with older software (Access 97, for example, will not read a database saved in Access 2000 format). This is another argument for standardizing on a particular version, as it is important in a library environment that users be able to share files.

If you use Outlook as your e-mail and productivity software, be sure to be on the alert for viruses and worms transmitted by e-mail. (See more on protecting your users from such threats in the Security section later in this chapter.) Outlook and Outlook Express are particularly likely to fall prey to these threats due to two factors: they contain security holes not necessarily present in other e-mail programs, and Microsoft presents an irresistibly large target for the creators of these exploits. This problem requires you to educate your library's staff on safe e-mail usage and to keep your software patched and updated.

Lastly, although Netscape Navigator formerly predominated in the library browser market, many institutions have now switched to using Internet Explorer (IE) on staff and public workstations. (Although Mozilla has made some inroads, IE is the browser of choice in most institutions due to its being preloaded on the desktop, the instability of later versions of Netscape, IE's tight integration with Windows, and pre-existing patron and staff familiarity with its use.) Using IE on public workstations in the library creates a particular set of challenges. Since the software is primarily intended for home use, it can be difficult to lock down in a library environment, preventing multiple users from changing settings, adding plugins, and altering the software for their own purposes. Any systems administrator looking to lock down IE should investigate Andrew Mutch's pages at http://tln.lib.mi.us/~amutch/pro/ie. (Mutch also provides information on his pages on locking down other commonly used browsers.) Also see the section on security later in this chapter, and look at Microsoft's Internet Explorer Administration Kit, which provides additional tools for customizing and locking down the browser. One last option is to turn to Public Web Browser, which, although based on IE, is specifically intended for use in a public environment. See http://teamsoftware.bizland.com/projects.htm.

Since Microsoft products are so predominant, resources on their use are also abundant. Beyond the official Microsoft support site and knowledge base at http://support.microsoft.com, you may wish to investigate the following:

- *Woody's Watch* (http://www.woodyswatch.com): Free e-mail newsletters containing straightforward advice, tips, and tricks on Office, Windows, Access, and other products.

- *Windows Annoyances* (http://www.annoyances.org): Tips on customizing Windows, Windows usage, and getting rid of annoyances. Also features downloads and discussions.

Macintosh

Macintosh expertise will likely be required if you are taking (or developing) your systems skills to a school media center environment. The K–12 market is one of the few significant remaining strongholds for the Mac, and many school libraries will be working with a mixture of legacy Macintosh hardware and newer Macs such as eMacs, iMacs, or G4s, as well as with PCs. This will also be a good time to brush up on the intricacies of Macintosh–PC networking, including using AppleTalk, and on file conversion and sharing between the two platforms. Each of these presents its own set of challenges.

If you are adding new equipment, be wary of mixing PCs and Macs in your computing environment. While doing so may on the surface seem to provide optimum flexibility for users, this one advantage is outweighed by the potential for confusion among computer users, compatibility issues, and the additional headaches supporting both platforms will create.

The main source of support for Macintosh products is of course Apple's support site at http://www.apple.com/support, which links you to the company's knowledge base, online forums, and so on. Other useful support sites include:

- *MacFixIt.com* (http://www.macfixit.com): Online forums, Weblog, troubleshooting reports, and downloads.

- *Macworld* (http://www.macworld.com): The companion site to Macworld magazine includes product reviews, news, and discussion forums.

- *TidBITS* (http://www.tidbits.com): Includes an e-newsletter, forums, and site devoted to Mac issues.

Open Source Software

Open source software (OSS) is gaining a stronger following in the library community, as pricing, security, and philosophical considerations provide an impetus for considering alternatives to Microsoft's dominance. The open source movement shares a great deal with the philosophy of librarianship, most notably an emphasis on the sharing of information and enabling users to find resources and resolve problems on their own. As Eric Lease Morgan writes: "In general, librarianship is an honorable profession and people are drawn to the profession because of a sense of purpose, a desire to provide service to the community. While many open source software developers create applications to solve local, real-world problems, their efforts are shared because they desire to give back to the community. Do you remember the Internet saying from about 10 years ago? 'Give back to the 'Net.' That saying lives on in open source software and is manifested in the principles of librarianship."[2] Librarians and open source proponents share a sense of the value of community and of resource sharing that seems to make them natural partners.

So, what defines open source software? Most software from traditional vendors is completely proprietary, down to its source code (which is closely guarded and unable to be modified). Open source alternatives allow free and open access to the source code, under the assumption that the wider programming community can improve and adapt the software faster than any conventional programming team. This results in a process similar to peer review, in which unusable projects sink under the weight of community criticism and useful examples shine—and benefit from others' input. Examples of major and popular open source applications include the Apache Web server, openoffice.org, Perl, Mozilla, and Linux. Much open source software is released under the GNU General Public License (GPL), which provides terms for using, distributing, and freely modifying software. (View the current version of the GPL at http://www.gnu.org/copyleft/gpl.html.)

Useful resources and background material for library OSS proponents include:

- OSSNLibraries, a directory and webliography of projects and resources at http://dewey.library.nd.edu/ossnlibraries/portal.

- The oss4lib Web site (http://www.oss4lib.org) and e-mail discussion list (http://www.oss4lib.org/listserv)

include information on a number of OSS projects, downloads, and news.

- Eric Lease Morgan's "OSSNLibraries – Open Source
  Software 'N Libraries" is an online version of a presentation he made at the 2001 ALA annual conference. See
  http://www.infomotions.com/musings/ossnlibraries.
  shtml.

- The Open Source Initiative, at http://www.opensource.
  org.

- Raymond, Eric S. *The Cathedral and the Bazaar: Musings
  on Linux and Open Source by an Accidental
  Revolutionary*. O'Reilly & Associates, rev. ed. 2001.

- Sisler, Eric. "Linux in the Library." Accessible online:
  http://gromit.westminster.lib.co.us/linux/linux-
  library.html.

- *Information Technology and Libraries*, 21:1 (March 2002).
  Special theme issue on open source software, with
  selected articles accessible online: http://www.lita.
  org/ital/ital2101.html.

Open source proponents also emphasize the potential cost savings of using free and open source software. Keep in mind, however,
that you will need to factor in the total cost of ownership, which
may include a higher learning curve that can result in the need for
additional training, the lack of formal or centralized support and
documentation, and the necessity for your library to hire someone
with the knowledge to maintain these systems when you leave (or
the willingness to acquire such knowledge). These factors may well
be balanced by the absence of prohibitive licensing schemes and
the ability to move away from reliance on large outside vendors, but
this is an informed decision you will need to make in conjunction
with your library's administration. (For more on open source software and library automation, see Chapter 8.) If you do choose to

use open source products, be prepared to make the commitment to hands-on involvement with customizing and learning the software.

Blake Carver's Modifications of Ranganathan's Rules[3]

1. Software is for use

2. Every computer its users

3. Every reader his source code

4. Save the time of the user

5. A system is a growing organism

When researching open source software, realize the following:

- Open source alternatives, although sometimes free and often lower cost than proprietary solutions, are not necessarily without cost.

- Open source may require a greater commitment from you and/or your department in terms of staff training and support, due to a potentially higher learning curve and the lack of complete documentation.

- Some open source projects, especially those that stem largely from a single developer, run the risk of the developer's losing interest (or funding) and ceasing to support or develop an application.

The above is not meant to warn you off the use of open source alternatives. Rather, you may wish to implement open source in your library with a cautious awareness of potential pitfalls. You may choose to add and test open source tools to increase the

functionality of existing applications, or to use them in conjunction with existing proprietary software before diving into a fully
open source environment. (Find a number of such tools on http://
www.oss4lib.org.) The low cost and low system requirements of a
lot of open source software provides room for experimentation.
You might use an older machine that is slated for discard to install
and experiment with Linux, for example.

You might choose to use an open source Weblog tool to allow
library staff to share comments and news on your institution's
intranet. You may choose to install Apache as your Web server
software rather than relying on alternatives from Microsoft and
other vendors, investigate customizing MyLibrary@NCState to add
personalization features to your Web site, or to look into using
Mozilla for your public Internet stations and OpenOffice.org on
your public office machines. Also note that a number of commonly
used library-specific tools, such as the Prospero Web-based document delivery add-on to Ariel, and OCLC SiteSearch, are already
open source. The widespread adoption of such tools by libraries
provides you with a built-in community of colleagues to assist you
with any issues in implementation or usage. Further, if you have
created a locally used software add-on, script, or tool, consider
releasing it to the library community at large. This serves the dual
goals of assisting others while opening up room for feedback from
those who implement your solution, giving you the opportunity to
improve your tool.

Networking

Networking in libraries can encompass a variety of issues; as
always, networking depends on the needs and technological environment of your institution. In all but the smallest library, you will
likely at least be involved with administering an Internet-connected
local area network (LAN). At a minimum, this network requires

ensuring that the server(s) stay up, that users can access the Internet, and that the client machines (whether there are 5 or 500 of these) can connect to the server and access shared resources such as files and printers. Depending on your institutional environment, you also may be involved in ensuring the security of your network through deployment of a hardware or software firewall, while ensuring that the firewall is also flexible enough to allow authorized access to online subscription databases and other desired resources. (In larger or consortial environments the firewall may be maintained at the system's end.)

Software packages such as Microsoft Office may also be installed on your server and accessed from the client machines, rather than installed and used from the hard drive of each client. Shared CD-ROM products can sometimes be copied to a shared network hard drive and accessed throughout the library. (Although most library CD products are moving to Internet-accessible resources, some are still available only on CD-ROM, or your institution may wish to provide access to legacy products as well as to newer online subscriptions.) Decisions on what to make available through your network will depend largely on the size and needs of your library and the reliability of your network server and connections.

Most libraries currently employ some form of Ethernet network, with some institutions moving toward replacing or supplementing standard Ethernet cabling with fiber or wireless connections. This network may be small enough to run off of one Windows NT or 2000 server, or it may employ multiple servers and server software packages (including Linux, Unix, and Novell NetWare as well as products from Microsoft). Larger libraries, especially in a university setting, may be more likely to utilize Unix on their servers than smaller institutions. If your Web site and/or e-mail server is locally hosted, you will need to support Internet services as well as local functions on your network. You may also wish to set up related locally hosted services such as e-mail lists or newsletters for your staff and/or patrons.

Client machines may be full-fledged workstations running a client OS such as Windows 2000 Professional, or they may be "thin client" machines that only gain functionality when connected to your network. Your building(s) may be new enough to have been wired when built, or you may need to run Ethernet cable to each client location as needed. (There are a number of companies with which you can contract to do your site's wiring, which may be better for network continuity and throughput than trying to run and crimp cable yourself if you are not familiar with doing so.) If you need to add cabling and additional workstations, you may also be involved in planning for new wiring centers, or at a minimum adding switches to expand the number of clients you can support. Here, you will also need to be cognizant of licensing issues—on a Microsoft-based network, for example, you will need to purchase a client access license for each additional workstation you connect to your server. If you are interviewing for a systems librarian position, be sure to ask questions about the type and size of network you may be responsible for supporting.

Wireless technologies, while still fairly new in libraries, are beginning to catch on as a useful way of avoiding the annoyance of running cable to every place you may wish to drop a network node. In a wireless environment, infrared or radio signals are used to transmit network data between network nodes and a wireless access point (which works much like a traditional network hub), allowing you to place workstations and other devices with wireless network adapters throughout your building—and move them around without having to drop new cable. Wireless networks can also be combined with existing wired versions, providing an alternative method of network expansion. While wireless technology is still somewhat more expensive to install than traditional Ethernet cabling, the price is coming down, and the flexibility it allows may compensate for the initial cost differential. (You may also see wireless networks referred to as 802.11b networks, after the currently most common wireless standard.)

Useful resources for those interested in establishing wireless LANs in libraries include:

- Bill Drew's Wireless Librarian page, at http://people. morrisville.edu/~drewwe/wireless/, which contains links to vendor information, article citations and links, and an e-mail discussion list on the subject.

- "Wireless: LANS" is a PLA Tech Note by Richard W. Boss, which summarizes the state of wireless technology and how public libraries are using it. Available online at http://www.pla.org/publications/technotes/technotes_ lans.html.

- Glover, James L. "Look Ma, No Wires! Or the Ten Steps of Wireless Networking." *Computers in Libraries*, March 2001. Accessible online: http://www.infotoday.com/ cilmag/mar01/glover.htm.

If you are considering creating a wireless LAN in your institution, also be aware of the potential security implications. Be sure to invest in devices that at least subscribe to the Wireless Encryption Protocol (WEP) and that provide a sufficient level of encryption to protect users' data—and be sure to turn that encryption on! (It is generally not turned on by default.) Change default names, set passwords, and realize that it is easier for library patrons to access your system illegally if they do not physically have to connect to an Ethernet port. There has been recent discussion as to whether WEP is sufficient to protect wireless networks, so, before deploying your wireless LAN, read up on the current state of encryption and decide whether this technology is suitable for your situation.

Related to wireless networking is the newer issue of using handheld devices such as personal digital assistants (PDAs) or

Web-enabled mobile phones in a library environment. If this is a possibility for your library, check out "The Handheld Librarian" Weblog at http://www.handheldlib.blogspot.com. Uses of handhelds in libraries include online catalog and electronic database access, platforms for e-books, and presentation platforms. Medical libraries are beginning to look at providing information to healthcare professionals at patients' bedsides through handheld devices loaded with medical databases and reference books; see for example http://pdagrant.osfsaintfrancis.org. Some libraries are investigating checking out handhelds to patrons or providing content for users' existing PDAs through AvantGo channels and similar methods. (For an example of a vendor actively working to bring a readable OPAC to the mobile screen, see information on Innovative Interfaces' AirPAC at http://www.iii.com/pdf/airpac.pdf.)

Related networking issues involve providing consistent access to your library's community, whether users are on- or off-site. Your library or consortium may choose, for example, to run remote requests for access to IP-restricted licensed databases through a proxy server so that you can authenticate such requests against your patron database (or by username and password). Proxy servers permit remote access by handling remote requests and passing them through to vendor databases as if the requests were originating from an IP address within your network. Software proxies such as EZproxy that run on an institution's server (bypassing any requirement for users to make modifications to the proxy settings in their individual browser software) are popular in libraries of all types, and also allow you to gather statistics on remote usage of your electronic resources. (See more information on EZproxy at http://www.usefulutilities.com/ezproxy.) Some integrated library system (ILS) vendors also provide their own remote authentication products, such as Epixtech's Remote Patron Authentication. (See http://www.epixtech.com/products/rpa.asp.)

Lastly, you might be involved in creating a virtual private network (VPN) environment for library staff if you have a number of telecommuters or others needing to access local resources from remote locations. A VPN allows users coming in over the Internet to be recognized as if they were coming from within the local network, while adding encryption to protect your institution's data while it is being transmitted over the public Internet. In this way, a cataloger working from home that logs into your VPN, for example, can be allowed access to Telnet in and modify item records in your ILS database just as if she were working on location at your institution.

Web Design

Libraries have been creating institutional Web sites since the graphical Internet first began to catch on, extending their traditional roles as disseminators and organizers of information. While such sites started as static collections of information about the library's hours, services, and so on, many libraries have taken advantage of newer Web technologies and techniques to move into creating dynamically generated sites, housing digital collections, providing off-site access to electronic subscription resources, and so on.

Due to the changing nature of library sites, Web librarians have experienced a corresponding change in duties and expectations. Whereas many librarians began creating and maintaining their library's Web presence on an ad hoc basis, with just a minimal knowledge of HTML or of entry-level editors such as Microsoft FrontPage, the rising expectations of Internet users and the ability to facilitate the library's mission through interactive technologies have raised the bar in many institutions. Many library Web designers now face multiple challenges, ranging from the need to provide sites that meet users' rising expectations while still remaining accessible to users with disabilities, the onus for creating a selection policy for links, the need to make tough decisions as to which parts of the enterprise will be emphasized on the library's front page, and the necessity of supporting more advanced technologies such as database-driven sites, personalization, distance learning portals, and streaming Webcasts.

Webmasters in many institutions today, therefore, need to acquire skills ranging from programming and database design to graphics creation and animation. Beyond basic HTML, you may also need to familiarize yourself with XML, ASP, XHTML, and other functions such as CSS. Tangential, and not specifically technical, issues to familiarize yourself with as a library Webmaster include online copyright and privacy issues and developing linking and public Internet usage policies.

Any aspiring Web librarian should bookmark the Library Web Manager's Reference Center (http://sunsite.berkeley.edu/Web4Lib/RefCenter), which complements the Web4Lib e-mail discussion list. Also examine A List Apart at http://alistapart.com, and Metronet's links for library Webmasters at http://www.metronet.lib.mn.us/libpage/links.cfm, as well as Innovative Internet Applications in Libraries at http://www.wiltonlibrary.org/innovate.html.

You may also be involved in creating an intranet for library staff to facilitate access to internal resources. This intranet can be hosted on your internal network server and made accessible only to staff machines. This is a useful way to post and share staff documents such as personnel codes and library policies, training materials, answers to commonly asked reference questions, and schedules and calendars. If you wish guidance on creating an intranet in your own library, refer to the PLA TechNote on Intranets at http://www.pla.org/publications/technotes/technotes_intranet.html.

Integrated Library System Management

Integrated library system (ILS) management is one area in which your library background will be essential. Without an understanding of cataloging fundamentals, for example, it is nearly impossible to understand the ILS needs of a cataloging department. As survey respondent Marc Truitt, head, library systems department at the University of Notre Dame Libraries notes: "Most of my previous training and experience was in technical services, especially acquisitions and cataloguing. These have proven invaluable in my current job of supporting a library ILS. They also enable me to understand much better the perspectives of staff trying to accomplish technical services functions in an automated environment. We can talk with each other and I sense that the folks on the production end of things not only recognize that I understand their concerns and needs, but that I *sympathize* with them on another level entirely." (For a discussion of the issues involved in planning an ILS migration, see Chapter 8.)

Managing an ILS requires attention to issues as varied as:

- Regular backups of patron and bibliographic data

- Maintaining the ILS server and database

- Creating and running reports

- Technical support for ILS users

- Customizing the display of your public-access catalog

- Managing access to and setting up security for staff modules

- Installing client software on staff workstations

- Serving as the liaison between your library and the ILS vendor

- Keeping current with new versions and features, and coordinating any needed upgrades

- Testing connections between the ILS and any linked external databases

- Setting up policies in conjunction with other library staff

- Implementing new or additional modules

In many cases, ILS management will be carried out largely by staff at your library system or consortium, and you will serve as their local liaison. In a stand-alone library, however, someone needs to take responsibility for each of the areas in the preceding list, as well as for any other ILS issues that may arise.

Troubleshooting

As is true of all electronic equipment, computer components and hardware inevitably fail, experience glitches, and require upgrading in order to take advantage of more current technology. Especially if you are in a larger institution with hundreds of workstations, sending machines out for repair or upgrade whenever needed can become prohibitively expensive and time-consuming. Luckily, many common tasks, from adding RAM to swapping cables to installing network cards, are easily mastered. A willingness to tinker is often all that is needed to give you a solid background in maintaining computer hardware and resolving hardware issues.

As academic systems librarian Terry Ballard noted even back in 1994, "When a piece of equipment is broken, the only procedure is to send it out for repair. However, I have found that only one percent of my cases need to be sent out. As someone with no technical background and little formal education in computer science, I feel pretty good about that score. The point is not that I am an

extraordinary troubleshooter—it's that if I can learn to do this anybody can."[4]

You can begin hardware troubleshooting with a fairly basic set
of tools; for many jobs, all you will need is a Philips screwdriver. If
you find you often need to delve into your machines' innards, you
may wish to invest in a small computer technician's toolkit, flash-
light, and other basics. Familiarize yourself with the basic layout of
PCs; take the time to open a case and explore before you need to
do so in an emergency. You can use older, discarded machines to
practice on or to strip for parts—and newer PCs are often lighter,
easier to open, and better-laid-out, which means that working on
them will be a breeze if you have learned on older machines.

You will also need to become comfortable troubleshooting common problems with computer software and configurations. (Find
more on researching such issues in Chapter 4.) Some preventative
maintenance will go a long way toward preventing many system
problems, as will regular backups or drive imaging. On Internet-
connected terminals, make a habit of removing spyware and
adware with a program such as Ad-Aware (http://www.lsfileserv.
com), as these unwanted programs can make machines run slug-
gishly after a while. Defragment disks, back up Windows registries,
and otherwise make a habit of maintaining your PCs. Much of this
can be automated to run at night if you are in a network environment, when it will be least disruptive to staff and patrons.

If you are in a large, spread-out institution, or if you have WAN
responsibilities, look into remote-access software such as PC
Anywhere or its free competitor, VNC. These programs will allow
you to access both your server and clients from your own desktop,
saving you the time and trouble of having to physically visit a malfunctioning workstation or needing to sit at the server to make
configuration changes or add users.

Programming

While programming skills are a luxury in many smaller institutions, in larger environments, or in those requiring home-grown solutions, some programming knowledge will be useful. Whether you are writing original scripts to extend the functionality of your ILS or adding Java personalization features to your Web page, programming skills can be useful to many institutions. More systems librarian job ads are now specifying some sort of programming or scripting expertise, particularly knowledge of Web technologies and related languages such as Java and ASP.NET. Evaluate the market and the type of library you wish to work in before making a significant investment in shoring up your programming skills, but realize that there are situations in which such skills will come in handy.

Antivirus and Workstation Security

In an open environment such as a library, ensuring the security of the computing environment is integral to the smooth functioning of library systems. Whether by accident or by design, patrons are prone to wreaking havoc with unprotected machines, changing settings, releasing viruses, deleting files, or saving pornographic images to the desktop. Since PCs by default assume that their users have certain access to their machine, it is incumbent upon you to prevent such problems by locking down public workstations, protecting them from patron interference.

Start by setting a BIOS password on all machines, and set all of your public PCs to boot off of the hard drive before accessing a floppy drive. Your attempts at locking down a Windows desktop, for example, will be futile if users can simply insert a system disk into drive A: and boot to a command prompt.

There are a number of methods of desktop control, which may be used alone or in combination, as appropriate to your situation.

You may also wish to use these methods in conjunction with software such as Norton's Ghost or PowerQuest's DeployCenter (formerly Drive Image Pro), which allow for easy imaging and restoration of workstations. Another option is to invest in a program such as Fortres' Clean Slate or Hyper Technologies' Deep Freeze, each of which restores your original system configuration, settings, and files on each reboot. Such software might be most useful in a computer lab environment, when you wish to allow access to Windows functions for training purposes but still want to keep users from permanently damaging settings or configurations.

The first approach to securing public machines is to invest in a license for security software such as Fortres 101 or Hyper Technologies' WINSelect POLICY, which locks unauthorized users out of such danger zones as "My Computer" and the Windows Start menu. Realize that you will have to do some configuring so that Fortres (or your product of choice) will allow access to the programs and services you do want patrons to be able to use. You should be able to install security software on your server and configure group settings, saving the trouble of creating new settings for each machine you wish to protect. Another option is Bardon Data Systems' WinU, which replaces the Windows desktop with a menu that allows access only to pre-chosen programs. For public Macintosh stations, investigate software such as FoolProof Security for Mac OS (http://www.smartstuff.com/fps/fpsmac.html). Such security software has been discussed at length on Web4Lib and Syslib-L; search the archives of these lists for testimonials and warnings. (Find information on lists in Chapter 5.)

You might also decide to control access to the desktop through setting network rights and permissions for certain users and groups. Use group policies, for example, to lock patron logins out of changing settings, and/or limit their logins to accessing only a single program (such as Internet Explorer on catalog terminals or Internet stations). It should go without saying that you need to discourage library staff from leaving staff passwords on display or making their passwords simple to guess. Add-on software packages from vendors such as Fortres and Hyper Technologies also allow you to "gray out" program menu options, preventing users, for example, from changing software settings via built-in menus. Create written policies for your institution that delineate what users will be allowed to do on public machines; you will probably, for example, wish to disallow loading of personal software onto library workstations.

Security software or network policies, however, are insufficient protection for your workstations. Protect each computer in your building, as well as your network server, with reputable antivirus software, and be sure to keep your virus definitions updated daily. (You should be able to download definitions onto your server and then update workstations from the local network.) Major antivirus vendors include Symantec (Norton Antivirus), Network Associates (McAfee), and Frisk International (F-Prot). Invest in a site license or in sufficient client licenses to protect all of your machines. With the proliferation of e-mail-borne viruses, you may also wish to protect staff machines from infection by stripping off any executable file attachments (such those with .exe, .pif, and .bat extensions) at the mail server end. Staff should have no reason to be receiving files of this type, and removing such attachments before they are received will go a long way toward protecting your network. Be sure also to set your virus scanner to check all floppy drives on access, as this is another major method of infection.

While software security is important, also recognize the necessity of protecting the physical security of your equipment. Consider the possibility of equipment theft, especially if your library is open late and/or understaffed. If this is an issue for your institution, you may wish to invest in lock-down cables to prevent users from removing expensive printers, monitors, and CPUs. Users in some libraries have been known even to steal the balls out of unprotected mice, and staff members have resorted to gluing them shut (although this makes cleaning them difficult) or have switched to optical versions. Protect against power surges with UPS/surge protectors at each workstation, if possible. Create emergency startup disks for your workstations, and back up important data. This is less of an issue on public machines where users should not be storing personal data in the first place (use your security software or network policies to disable saving to any drive but the floppy), but staff should be encouraged to save all documents to network drives, which should be backed up each night. Check the integrity of your network backup on a regular basis by attempting to restore files off tape, to ensure that your data has not been corrupted and that files are actually backing up.

Miscellaneous Issues

You may also be called upon to support a number of newer and more library-specific technologies and services in your institution. These include:

- *E-book distribution.* Issues here include the selection of platforms and formats the library will support, assisting the cataloging department in deciding when and how to catalog e-books, delivering content to handheld devices, and deciding when and how to circulate e-books.

- *Digitization projects.* Digitization encompasses a variety of issues, discussion of which could easily fill up an entire volume. Libraries involved in digitization projects are most often concerned with preserving and making available historical materials. A sampling of what you may need to concern yourself with here includes the process of converting documents, photographs, and/or videos to digital format, creating cataloging records and metadata, ensuring accessibility, storage, and usability, and attending to the copyright protection and adherence of your digitized collections. RLG DigiNews is a good resource for digital library managers: http://www.rlg.org/preserv/diginews.

- *Distance learning.* If the university in which your library is located provides distance learning opportunities to its students, your library will need to provide distance learning support for these classes. This can include anything from creating Web pages and providing and promoting online resources, to electronic reserves, to snail-mailing course materials to students enrolled in distance-learning courses, to supporting interactive courseware.

- *Virtual reference services.* Virtual reference is starting to catch on at larger and university libraries, as a way of providing reference services to patrons who are not physically on library premises and/or to fulfill the promise of 24/7 access. Virtual reference services can range from supporting e-mailed reference questions to implementing a live environment involving chat and the ability to "push" Web sites and other resources to remote users. The latter requires your attention to details ranging from selecting and setting up software and Web pages, to training reference staff to interact in the online environment, to managing logs gathered from such live interactions. Consult Bernie Sloan's Digital Reference Services Bibliography, online at http://www.lis.uiuc.edu/~b-sloan/digiref.html, for a number of resources on virtual reference.

- *Electronic resource licensing and management.* Your duties here can range from selecting subscription

databases, to negotiating license agreements with vendors, to training staff and patrons on the use of various
resources, to arranging on- and off-site access to a variety
of databases. Newer ideas include supporting the integration of multiple resources into one Web-based interface,
using tools such as OCLC's SiteSearch (https://www.site-
search.oclc.org) or WebFeat (http://www.webfeat.org). In
larger institutions, you might want to be able to create
reports and identify which full-text database contains a
desired journal by using tools such as Serials Solutions
(http://www.serialssolutions.com). When selecting and
maintaining electronic resources for your library, always
remember that, although formats may change, your
goal is to provide library users with the information
and resources that will be most useful to them.

- *Public Internet access.* See the Microsoft section earlier in
  this chapter for a brief discussion on deploying Web
  browsers in a public environment. Beyond the browser,
  however, systems librarians supporting public Internet
  access must make decisions varying from which plugins
  to install and support, to what headphones to buy that
  will be both sanitary and unlikely to break easily, to
  whether to allow access to chat, gaming, and similar
  activities, to how often and how extensively to offer
  patron training. Internet filtering is a separate issue that
  is beyond the scope of this book, but realize that you
  might be involved both in discussions with your administration and/or the public on filtering's advisability and
  effectiveness and in implementing a filtering solution,
  should your library choose to use one. Many libraries
  will also choose to implement some sort of time metering
  and/or print management software, which you will also
  need to research and support.

- *Adaptive technologies.* Public and university libraries have
  a responsibility to provide open access to all users, and

part of providing such access is making library computer technology accessible to all. Your institution might, for example, invest in screen reader or zooming software for the visually impaired. You will wish to ensure that at least some of your workstations are wheelchair-accessible—do not locate all of your catalog and electronic resource stations at stand-up carrels.

- *Mobile Access.* A number of libraries have begun extending the traditional concept of the bookmobile to include "cybermobiles," which can provide roving Internet access, computer training classes, and online database access from the road. You will need to research connectivity options such as satellite Internet access or cellular modem solutions.

- *Personalized Web Portals.* MyLibrary (originally from North Carolina State) and similar products allow the library's Web users to set up a personalized profile. They can customize the home page to fit their needs and interests, for example, limiting electronic databases to those useful to their own course of study, keeping track of items checked out and on hold, and so on.

The preceding descriptions, while insufficient to describe all a systems librarian's job truly entails, should give you an idea of the common tasks and background shared by many. If you are thinking of becoming a systems librarian, consider whether you have an existing aptitude for, knowledge of, or willingness to learn more about one or more of these areas. Try not to be intimidated by the sheer variety of tasks described above; you will not need to be an expert in every area, and much depends on the needs of your particular institution.

Works Cited

1. Krug, Steve. *Don't Make Me Think: A Common Sense Approach to Web Usability.* Indianapolis: New Riders Publishing, 2000: 148.

2. Morgan, Eric Lease. "OSSNLibraries – Open Source Software in Libraries." 8 June 2001, modified 11 June 2001. February 2, 2002. (http://www.infomotions.com/musings/ossnlibraries.shtml).

3. Blake Carver is the creator of LISNews.com (http://www.lisnews.com). Rules reproduced with permission.

4. Ballard, Terry. "Zen in the Art of Troubleshooting." *American Libraries*, January 1994: 110.

Chapter 3

Organization of Knowledge

"The bottom line here is that yes, statistics are useful, but you shouldn't worship them. They are like a slightly out-of-focus snapshot of what you do, taken through glass that's distorted and not quite clean."

—Michael Schuyler[1]

Many noncatalogers look back on their required cataloging courses with a mingled sense of relief and disbelief. The organization of human knowledge, however, remains one of the foundations of librarianship, and, whether or not we retain a personal fondness for the intricacies of the MARC record, most librarians do love order. Cultivate the ability to organize the IT knowledge of your own department or organization, which will always stand you in good stead. The very process of working in the computer field will make you realize the importance of being able to put your hands quickly on the correct piece of information, whether you are looking for vendor contact information, system configurations, license numbers and registration keys, documentation, or any of the multitude of other details involved in managing technology in libraries.

Each institution will have its own mix of hardware, software, and other computer technology, as well as varying levels of complexity in keeping accurate track of technological resources. It is not necessary to catalog your technology holdings in full MARC format, but, whether you keep your records entered in a variety of databases or written down and filed in manila folders, some type of organizational system is necessary. The following pages contain suggestions on record keeping and statistics collection that will be necessary in all libraries; you can modify these requirements or methods of organization to fit your own institution's needs. Find discussions on inventorying computer systems, tracking software licenses, maintaining support information, keeping good statistics on electronic usage, and creating useful documentation for others.

Inventorying

Maintaining an accurate tally of your computing assets will be necessary for a number of reasons. First, when you are creating a technology or strategic plan for your institution, you will need to be able to paint a complete picture of your library's current computing environment. (For more on technology plans, see Chapter 8.) If you have not made a habit of keeping accurate records that describe how computer equipment and software are being deployed throughout your institution as these products and services are added, then you will need to conduct an inventory from scratch when the time comes to compose your planning documents. Maintaining an ongoing inventory (that can be modified whenever you purchase or modify computer hardware or software) will simplify the planning process and allow you to see an outline of your technology holdings at a glance.

You also may be required to keep an inventory of computer equipment as part of your library's annual audit. An auditor will need to be told, and perhaps be shown, the locations of all major computer equipment you purchase during a given year—to ensure that these purchases are actually being made for and used by your library. In a larger institution where it is less easy to spot a newer item after the fact, it will be necessary to keep accurate records of where in your library you have installed or replaced hardware during any given year and to be able to match up your inventory with purchase orders and invoices.

Each piece of equipment and each computer system in your institution can be labeled with an inventory number, which can also be kept with invoices, documentation, and maintenance histories for easier match up. Any method that allows you to locate equipment quickly and to match it up with its information and invoices will suffice. Other advantages accrue to those willing to maintain inventory records. An ongoing inventory will also help you, for example, to keep track of the library's computing environment and to know where and when you need to update, upgrade, or replace hardware and software. If you keep maintenance records as part of your inventory, you will be able to recognize at a glance which machines have been behaving poorly. You can identify how many printers you have in a particular make and model, which will help determine how many of a particular toner cartridge you may wish to keep in stock. You can easily see when each machine was purchased, which helps you keep to a set replacement cycle and to tell at a glance if a machine is under warranty or a support contract. Although these points may seem minor, each piece of documentation is helpful for the smooth running of library technology and will save you time in the long run.

Licensing

You or your department's staff will likely be responsible for keeping track of software licenses purchased by your institution. It is a good practice to be able to ensure that your library is in compliance with licensing requirements for any software deployed in your library, which requires accurate record keeping as to the number of installations, licenses, versions, and locations of particular products. If you are using newer Microsoft products in your institution through open license agreements, you will also need to create a Microsoft Passport account and keep track of that user name and password, as well as the license and grant numbers for each piece of software your library uses. (Whatever you may think of Passport's privacy and security implications, it remains a necessary evil for open license customers and many other institutions using current Microsoft software. To minimize your exposure, and to ensure others have access to Passport records if you should leave your institution, you may wish to create a general library e-mail account on your own mail server and use it solely for such registrations. Do not use Hotmail; since it is a free service and must therefore place restrictions on storage space, you likely will not receive any important messages regarding your registration if you fail to check and clean out your mailbox daily.)

Grant and/or license numbers may also be necessary when you need to contact technical support on a particular piece of software. Network Associates, for example, requires a valid grant number before providing telephone "prime" support on its McAfee antivirus products. If your antivirus software fails, machines are infected, or your server is somehow failing to download and install regular updates, being able to contact tech support immediately requires you to be able to locate and provide this information.

Ensuring licensing compliance will also prevent your institution from running into legal problems in the future. Software associations and companies are not generally swayed by either claims of poverty or of ignorance, and it is your responsibility as a systems librarian to be sure that your library is in compliance. This is one reason (other than the obvious support and ethical issues) to be wary of allowing users to install and use their own software; they may not think to put the good of the institution above their own convenience. You may wish to conduct a regular audit of installed software; you should create a policy stating that only systems staff may install software. At the very least, require staff to clear software installations with the systems department, or with you, if there is no formal IT department, before adding any programs to their machines. It is important to get the backing of your administration on this issue; describing the consequences in terms of possible fines for licensing violations and potential damage to users' systems from illegal and unapproved software will help you make your point. (For more on ethical issues and systems librarianship, see Chapter 9.)

You may also be required to register software in order to activate it. While this process might seem merely to be an annoyance, especially if you need to register multiple installations, registering all software in your name will ensure you are on vendors' mailing lists for upgrades and related offers (as well as for unrelated offers and junk mail, but this is another issue!). Registration also allows vendors to inform you of patches and security issues with your software and of trials of new versions, and some vendors will even offer free online seminars or other "perks" for registered users. Macromedia, for example, which produces Dreamweaver, ColdFusion, Fireworks, and other Web design tools, informs registered users via e-mail about opportunities such as online design seminars and classes on creating database-driven Web sites. If you fail to register your products, you may miss out on useful training opportunities. (See more on independent study in Chapter 7.)

Lastly, keep careful track of any registration keys you may have for your purchased software. This is especially important if you have downloaded and registered software online. If the computer on which you have installed the registered version crashes, or if you migrate to newer hardware, you will need the key to reinstall and unlock the software. Often, especially if you have purchased shareware from smaller independent vendors, you cannot count on their records to be accurate if you need to contact them and request that they reissue such a key. Smaller vendors might even go out of business before you need them again, so keep your keys and registration numbers safe.

Support Information

Accurate record keeping is also crucial in being able to adequately support your library's technology. Beyond keeping track of where computer hardware and software are installed throughout your institution, it is useful to have system information handy for each machine—especially when you need to do an emergency reinstallation of hardware drivers or of Microsoft Windows. You will also need to know your systems' hardware specifications when upgrading to a newer OS, such as when you move from Windows 98 to Windows 2000, for example. This will allow you to research whether a system will be capable of running a new OS smoothly before you begin the actual installation process and to locate and install device drivers that will work in your new operating environment.

At a minimum, for each machine, keep track of items such as:

- Installed RAM

- Windows version and OEM number (or equivalent for alternate operating systems)

- Network card model and manufacturer

- Video card model and manufacturer

- Clock speed

- Purchase date and system manufacturer

- Sound card model and manufacturer

This information is most easily recorded when you first buy the machine, but much of it can be retrieved from the system information found in the Windows device manager (or equivalent in your OS). Also record IP addresses for each workstation, if these are set to be static, as well as those for your network printers—which will allow easier setup when installing that printer on a newly purchased system.

You can keep your system information in a database, or, if you are in a smaller institution, simply written down (or filled out in a pre-made Word template) and filed in a binder. Use your inventory number as your database key, or file system information in order by number for easy retrieval. It will also be useful to keep a running detailed list of any maintenance and troubleshooting that has been done on these machines; this will help you identify "problem children," see what has already been done, and keep track of how your time (and, if applicable, that of your staff) has been spent. (See the sidebar.)

Sample System Information Sheet: Microsoft Word and Microsoft Access Formats

Number: Date Purchased: Manufacturer:

RAM: Processor Speed: Location:

Windows Version: Windows OEM Number:

Hard Drive Model/Size:

Network Card:

Sound Card:

Modem:

Video Driver:

Printer(s):

Maintenance Record (Include date, problem, and resolution):

If you have the storage space, keep each computer system's driver software and manuals together in its motherboard box and label each with its inventory number. In this way, if you need to work on the system, you will have everything you need close at hand. In your motherboard box, you may also wish to keep boot disks, warranty information, and any other useful material for that system.

Beyond keeping support information close at hand for each machine, you will also wish to collocate your vendor contact information so that it is easily retrievable when you need to contact tech support. Make sure you have current phone numbers, Web site addresses, and e-mail support addresses for all of your major software and hardware vendors. Keep track of when and why you have needed to call each vendor, and print out or file for future reference any Web pages or e-mailed fixes and documentation they send you.

Statistics

Circulation statistics have long been a traditional measure of libraries' usage. In an Internet era, however, statistics on the usage of electronic resources and library public-access computer equipment are equally as important as, if not more important than, traditional counts. A patron accessing an online database, visiting your Web site, e-mailing a reference question, or spending an hour typing on an in-house word processor is using library resources, just as the patron who comes in to check out a book or ask a question at the reference desk is. In many libraries, electronic resources have replaced traditional print-based references; online full-text journal databases predominate, for example, rather than shelves of periodical indexes. Yet, libraries often lack an accurate picture of how these nontraditional resources are being used.

Given the costs of online database subscriptions and other computer-based resources, having statistics on their use (and on any increase in their use) will help justify their recurring expense. These statistics will also help you plan for the future, as you see which resources are being used most heavily and how usage patterns change over time. If an expensive resource sees little use, you can choose either to publicize its availability and offer training on its usage, or to cancel your subscription and replace it with a database that will be more useful to your patrons. If you are continually maxing out your allowed simultaneous connections to a resource, you may wish to invest in additional licenses. Statistics on electronic usage will also help you make decisions on which print resources to maintain; if users prefer the electronic editions, for example, do you wish to maintain both versions?

Keeping track of statistics generated by your integrated library system (ILS) will be another useful way of seeing how people are using the library in nontraditional ways. Perhaps in-person interlibrary loan (ILL) requests at the reference desk are down, for example, but are they being replaced by patron-generated requests through the OPAC? Take advantage of any statistics you are able to generate or retrieve and use them to plan your future path. Run regular reports against your ILS database to get a picture of how these patterns change over time.

Most database vendors will supply monthly usage reports for their products. Unfortunately, note that these reports are not standardized across vendors and resources, so it can be difficult to use these vendor-supplied numbers to make strict comparisons between databases. Typical measurements include:

- Number of queries or searches.

- Number of logins. (This may be broken down into in-house and remote logins. If your database vendor is unable to distinguish remote logins made through your proxy server from in-house connections, you may need to compile your own statistics.)

- Number of times users were denied access. If your license allows a limited number of simultaneous connections, this will give you an idea of whether you might need to increase your allowed level.

- Number of items retrieved. For example, these might be individual full-text articles or abstracts viewed.

- Number of citations displayed.

- Number of items retrieved, broken down by title.

- Number of items e-mailed.

- Number of items printed.

- Number of logins by time of day, day of week. This can be a useful way of seeing how your library is fulfilling the promise of 24/7 access and the use patrons are making of remote resources during nonlibrary hours.

- Amount of time used monthly.

If your vendor does not seem to provide statistics in a timely fashion, you may be able to create your own rough measures by logging the traffic that passes through your proxy server. While this method will not provide an accurate picture of finer measurements, for example, such as total numbers of searches and what types of articles are being accessed, it at least can let you know the number of times a database has been accessed from both inside and outside your institution. Before resorting to this as your only measurement, however, check with the vendor; some supply statistics only upon request.

When deciding how to compile statistics on electronic resource usage, you may find Joe Ryan's Library Statistics and Measures Web page useful (http://web.syr.edu/%7Ejryan/infopro/stats.html). His site compiles statistical guidelines from library-related organizations, article and monograph citations, and national and state statistical reports on libraries.

You also may wish to maintain statistics on the number of full-text journals the library provides access to through such electronic databases. Again, these numbers should be available upon request or regularly provided by the database vendor; they will help you demonstrate how the addition of electronic resources extends the library's physical collection. You should also be able to access (or maintain) lists of journal titles that are included in the databases so that patrons can see whether and where a particular source they are trying to access is available. If you have purchased separate subscriptions to individual online journals, keep track of how these are being used as well.

Keeping similar statistics on the usage patterns of your Web site will help you make the argument for additional funding when it comes time to devote more resources to your online presence. These statistics will also allow you to target your efforts to enhancing the areas that site visitors find most useful, or publicizing and reorganizing areas that receive little traffic. Patterns will be easier to track if you have first structured your Web site in a logical manner, as most major statistical packages such as WebTrends track usage by directory (among other methods). WebTrends and similar products form the information from your Web server's logs into useful reports; these are usually run monthly to give you a useful and standardized method of comparing the ups and downs in site usage. These packages also generally provide useful information on the browser and operating system versions your visitors are using, which will help you make decisions as to what browser versions to support when designing your library's site. WebTrends (see Figure 3.1) and other packages' reports are customizable, so you may need to work with your own reports or with your outside host to ensure that you are seeing the results that will be most useful for your purposes.

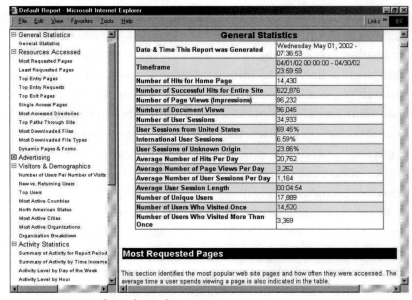

Figure 3.1   Sample WebTrends Report

If you have your site hosted at an external Web hosting company, note that most providers run a site analysis package on their servers and will be able to provide you with a URL from which you can access regular (generally monthly) reports. If you are hosting your site on your own server, you will need to invest in such a package. Investigate installing a free or low-cost log analyzer such as Analog (http://www.analog.cx) or Sawmill (http://www.sawmill.net).

See if the majority of your Web site traffic originates in-house or if you tend to serve large numbers of remote users. As patterns change and more visitors come from the outside, you might need to increase the number of resources you provide to off-site users. If you do not seem to be serving remote users, you may have a publicity problem and will need to work to get your site in search engines and directories as well as to increase awareness among your patron base of the resources accessible from outside your physical institution. Provide these numbers to your administration and your publicity and reference departments to help them make decisions on how best to publicize electronic resources.

If you have an internal site search function, keep track of what visitors are searching for. Tracking can give you ideas of commonly used areas you may wish to beef up or items you might wish to add to your site. It can also give you an indication as to whether your users are confusing your site search with general Internet search engines and whether you might need to more clearly describe your search box or link. Note that some free search services (such as Atomz.com, for sites less than 500 pages, and PicoSearch for sites less than 1,500) will keep search records and generate limited reports for you, but they usually require you to visit their site to generate a new index every time you make a change to your own Web pages. Find a number of options for site search tools for your Web site and/or intranet at http://www.searchtools.com.

When tracking your Web site usage, you may also wish to try to compile statistics on whether remote users are accessing your site via dialup modems or whether most of your community uses some type of broadband connection. For "soft" statistics of this type, you will likely need to survey your user population; consider posting such a survey on your Web site. Other uses for surveys include finding out whether users are actually retrieving what they need from your electronic databases, whether they are able to identify which database will be useful by referring to your online descriptions before starting their search, and whether they find the online help screens to be user-friendly.

Keeping track of patron use of remote resources also extends to tracking how they are using your ILS. Are patrons using the personalization features of your Web-based OPAC to check their accounts, place holds, and renew items? (If not, what can you do to publicize the availability of these services?) What percentage of your OPAC access stems from outside your institution? You may also be responsible for using built-in ILS capabilities to create and run reports for other departments on more traditional library usage measures, such as number of items circulated, number of patrons registered, and so on.

Public and academic libraries will wish to keep track of how public-access computers are being used within the library. If you use signup sheets for Internet access, for example, or if your time-management software compiles usage statistics, keep track of how many patrons use your Internet terminals on a monthly and yearly basis. (You might also wish to keep track of how many people are turned away or how often users must wait for a machine when all terminals are in use, which can help you see if additional stations might be needed.) If you teach public classes on basic Windows, Internet, and/or OPAC usage, keep track of how many people attend each. These numbers provide a rough measure as to whether you might need to add more terminals or classes. Keep track of how often patrons need computer help and if there are common questions that arise. This can let you see whether you need to create documentation answering frequently asked questions or increase staffing levels on certain days in computer labs or public service areas.

You may want (or be required) to keep other statistics, depending on the population your library serves. If you have a number of distance education students making use of library resources, for example, you will wish to track their use of automated ILL services and of any online e-mail or chat-based reference services that your institution offers, as well as tracking how many technical support questions IT staff handles from distance ed students. (Here, see whether there are common questions that may be better answered by composing an FAQ and making it available on the library's Web site or by providing a technical orientation at the beginning of distance learners' course of study.)

Documentation

Although you may not initially view the process of creating documentation for your library's computer systems and services in terms of the organization of knowledge, your efforts at documenting will in fact go a long way toward the effective organization and management of technology in your institution. Documentation in this sense includes organizing, collocating, and disseminating the knowledge that will help you and others succeed in your library's technological environment.

Creating useful documentation for general users requires an awareness of the mindset of those who might be using a particular piece of hardware or software for the first time. Construct your documentation in a clear, logical, manner, and be sure to provide step-by-step instructions for common tasks. Be liberal with screenshots so that users can follow along in pictures as well as with words to see if they are in the right place in your sequence of instructions. (See the "Sample Handout for Pasting a Resume into an Internet Form" sidebar for an example of a piece of such step-by-step documentation.) There are a number of low-cost share-ware screen capture programs that allow "capture with cursor" and the capture of sections of the screen; see for example SnagIt from http://www.techsmith.com. Basic word processing software such as Microsoft Word is sufficient to create printed documentation in most library environments.

Documentation will be useful for both library staff and library users, although it may take different formats and levels of complexity for your different audiences. For library users, consider creating "cheat sheets" on accomplishing specific, common tasks, such as attaching a resume to e-mail or looking up a title in your online catalog. You can supplement printed cheat sheets with more extensive online directions or direct users to resources (such as your catalog vendor's online help screens) and titles your library owns on using specific pieces of software.

Sample Handout for Pasting a Resume into an Internet Form

If you have your resume on a floppy disk in Microsoft Word format, and you are looking at a Web page where you would like to paste your resume into a form:

Step 1: Open and copy your resume

a) Put your disk in the A: (3½" floppy) drive on the Internet computer.

b) Minimize Internet Explorer by clicking on the "-" sign in the upper right-hand corner.

c) Open up the Microsoft Word Viewer by doubleclicking the icon on the desktop.

d) Microsoft Word Viewer will ask you what file you want to open. Switch over to the A: (3½" floppy) drive by clicking the drop-down arrow at the top of the screen and selecting 3½ Floppy A:

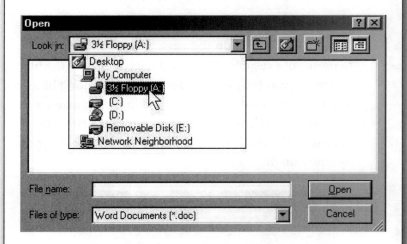

e) Once you are on the A: drive, you will see a list of the files on your disk. Select your resume file and click on Open.

f) Your resume file is now open in Microsoft Word Viewer.

g) Click on Edit near the top left of the screen. Click Select All. This should highlight your whole resume in blue.

h) Click Edit again and click on Copy. This will copy your whole resume into memory.

Step 2: Paste your resume onto the Internet

a) Click back over to Internet Explorer by choosing it in the bottom taskbar.

b) You should be back on the page where you were going to paste your resume. Make sure the cursor is in the box where you want to paste the resume in (look for it blinking inside the box). If it is not blinking, click inside the box with the left mouse button to put the cursor there.

c) Choose Edit, and click "Paste." This will paste your resume into the box.

d) Check to make sure that everything looks all right to you. Formatting such as • bullets, *italics*, and **boldface** will NOT show up. This is the time to look through what is pasted in the box and make any changes that you need.

For library staff, you can consider posting relevant documentation on your institution's intranet so that it is accessible to any staff member from any point inside the library. In a system or consortium where members use much of the same software, try collaborating with your peers in other institutions and sharing the documentation you create. There is no sense in reinventing the wheel if someone else has already produced a usable or easily modifiable document.

You will also wish to create a pool of documentation that you (and your systems staff) can draw upon. Document any support issues and their resolution so that if the situation again arises it can be dealt with quickly. Document server and network configurations, which will benefit you at a later date when you might not remember how you set up particular systems and will benefit any systems person who steps into your position if and when you decide to move on. Think of the information that would have made your job easier, and provide it for yourself, your staff, and your successor.

Overall, any organizational efforts you undertake have the main goal of making life simpler for yourself and your fellow staff members. As in the rest of systems work, your goal is to keep technology running smoothly and serving the good of the institution. Taking the time to keep track of how this is done will make everyone's job easier. Taken together, all of your documentation, statistics, maintenance, and inventory information provide a concrete pool of evidence for you to point to in describing the importance of your department's function to your institution. They paint a picture of what you have done and of the technological environment that needs supporting.

Works Cited

1. Schuyler, Michael. "Cutting-Edge Statistics." *Computers in Libraries*, March 2001: 53.

Chapter 4

Research Techniques

*"Knowing where to look for technology facts can be
very empowering; it can give you the confidence
that you can find an answer. As with reference
work, it is more important, and more possible, to
know where to look for technology information
than to know all the information yourself."*
— John J. Burke[1]

Systems librarians have an inherent advantage over IT personnel in nearly any other type of institution, for one simple reason:
we know how to find answers. The increasing complexity of computer systems and software ensures that no one person automatically possesses the right response for every situation. We rely on a
diversity of resources, from vendor knowledge bases, to our past
experiences with technology, to our colleagues in other institutions, to help us resolve technological issues, and to create usable
and useful computing environments for library staff and patrons.
In systems librarianship, as in librarianship in general, take heart
in remembering Mary Ellen Bates's maxim that: "Whatever the
question, you can either find the information or find someone
who can find it."[2]

Systems work and troubleshooting will give you a new apprecia-
tion for the way in which your library background builds a foundation for successfully finding and implementing technical
information. The usefulness of the experience you have built up in
areas such as online searching and reference work extends to systems work as well. As one survey respondent notes: "Reference/
searching skills have actually been most useful in troubleshooting.

It has never ceased to amaze me how much better I am at finding solutions to problems in knowledge bases (like Microsoft's) than my technical staff, most of whom, frankly, can barely spell." Thomas Reddick, automation coordinator at the Northeast Kansas Library System, concurs: "Frequently, I will find solutions that mere computer people cannot find."

Another advantage conveyed by a background in librarianship is the ability to critically evaluate the technical resources we find. We understand not only how to find information, but how to interpret and evaluate that information. When researching technical issues, you may uncover a great deal of misinformation and half-truths. Use your research techniques and skills to evaluate the reliability of any information you find, particularly online— where anyone can easily set himself up as a technical expert. Ask questions such as: Is the answer from a trusted source? Is it current? Does it match up with my existing store of knowledge about this product? Does it match up with my past experience? Can this information be verified with another source?

Our inherent skepticism and willingness to dig deeper can save us from acting on misinformation that may be not only unhelpful, but damaging to library equipment and software. Some recent Internet virus hoaxes, for example, have taken the form of e-mail suggesting that certain important system files, if present, are virus-infected, and advising users to delete such files—thereby crippling their own systems. Most librarians, even if they are newer to systems work, have developed critical thinking skills that prevent them from taking such rumors on face value. They should be able to consult authoritative sources to verify any such information before acting on it.

The sections in this chapter provide strategies and resources to help streamline your technical research and include information not only on where and how to locate answers, but on when and why research becomes necessary. There is an emphasis on Internet resources because these tend to be more up-to-date and because of the huge support community available online. Recognize, however, that opening up your support toolbox to include online resources requires that you give special attention to nurturing the critical thinking skills mentioned previously. Also in this chapter, you will find tips on dealing with vendor technical support as a last-ditch reference resource, conducting support interviews with your own users and staff to help determine the root of a given technical problem, and researching technology purchases.

Resources

The right mix of resources for locating solutions to your systems issues will be unique to your institution. You will want to maintain your own technical knowledge management environment, organizing and maintaining the resources that are likely to be most useful to you. Familiarize yourself with your selected resources and arrange them in a way that makes sense to you, in order to minimize the time you need to spend searching for answers to common problems later. Know which source is likely to contain the answer to specific types of problems.

Favorite Tech Support Resources: Systems Librarianship Survey

Respondents to the systems librarianship survey were each asked to list a favorite tech support resource. The overwhelming winning answers to this question emphasized the importance of building networks with others over any specific resource; the top three answers were some variation on e-mail lists, IT departments, and colleagues/staff. (For more on networking with others, see Chapter 5.) Many respondents did, however, mention specific resources (including specific lists). Here, online resources were clear favorites, and some top picks are listed below:

- *CNET*, at http://www.cnet.com, now owns both ZDNet and TechRepublic (see below). CNET.com itself provides technology information from a consumer perspective.

- *LIBNT-L* e-mail discussion list for Windows NT and 2000 administrators in library settings. Archives and subscription information at http://listserv.utk.edu/archives/libnt-l.html.

- *Microsoft Knowledge Base/Support/TechNet* at http://support.microsoft.com and http://www.microsoft.com/technet. Although various operating systems are in use in different library environments, Microsoft's overall predominance makes its site a favored destination. Realize also that you may find different answers at the support and TechNet sites; it is worth searching both on a particularly recalcitrant issue.

- *O'Reilly & Associates'* books and support site at http://www.ora.com. O'Reilly's solid print titles and thorough technical information mean that it has useful offerings for all library technical personnel.

- *SYSLIB-L*, an e-mail discussion list for systems librarians, provides online archives and a subscription form at http://listserv.acsu.buffalo.edu/archives/syslib-l.html.

- *TechRepublic.com* at http://www.techrepublic.com. This customizable online community for IT professionals provides tips, articles, news updates, discussion groups, downloads, e-mail newsletters, and more.

- *Web4Lib* e-mail discussion list for library Web managers. Information and archives available at http://sunsite.berkeley.edu/Web4Lib.

- *ZDNet* provides reviews, pricing, news, and downloads at http://www.zdnet.com, although it is more focused toward the general business user than CNET.

There are a number of important and commonly used resources that will be relevant to systems work in nearly every type and size of library. Supplement more general resources such as those listed in the sidebar with those specific to your institution's needs, such as your integrated library system (ILS) vendor's e-mail list and support Web site, any customized support pages for your system hardware, and those for your proxy, firewall, and/or filtering software vendors.

Online resources can be supplemented as well with more traditional print versions. Here again, you may have an existing advantage, as your institution likely already owns a number of computer books you can consult. Technical titles from O'Reilly & Associates and Que come highly recommended as solid resources for systems librarians, as do a number of the manuals from Neal-Schuman on issues more specific to libraries. When researching or learning more about a technical issue, also look for topical guides from your library associations—which have the advantage of being short, focused, and library-specific. LITA, for example, publishes monographs on topics from open source software for libraries to the usability of library Web sites (see http://www.lita.org/litapubs). Develop your own tech support bookshelf that you can turn to when your Internet access is down, or when it is easier to sit a book next to your terminal than to switch between screens when looking up answers online. At the very least, keep vendor documentation handy for each system and program, although this is now more often available only on CD-ROM or online. Check vendor documentation first in the event that yours is a common issue.

Techniques

When one of your systems has a tech support issue, you may find that dredging the right piece of information out of a balky online knowledge base, or locating an answer elsewhere, will be more difficult than you might expect. This becomes an increasing problem as software becomes more complex and as the number of (both known and unknown) issues grows. Many issues stem from the interaction of one vendor's piece of software with another vendor's product, so you will need to examine your operating environment as a whole when problems arise. If you have a failure in one program, it will often be due to a conflict with other software or hardware you have recently installed, so your first step might be to think about what changes you have recently made to a misbehaving system. Consult both the new vendor's and the older product's support information to see if there are known issues between the new product and your existing software. Also realize that the complexity of software and the sheer number of products out there can make navigating vendor Web sites treacherous at best. Microsoft.com alone, for example, is the fourth largest Web site in the world, and its organization (or lack thereof) reflects the difficulty of remaining consistent across this many documents.

Viewing support issues from a reference standpoint, however, can help you dissect these problems. First, you will need to get a handle on a good starting point for your search. As one survey respondent notes: "The system going down is not that different than someone coming to the reference desk with an in-depth question on a subject you've never heard of and have to ask them how to spell while they're explaining it." Is the system generating an error message? Write it down—or drag it out of the affected user—and do a search on the specific phrase or event ID number. Start with the vendor's online knowledge base. If you have had difficulty locating information in a poorly organized or badly indexed knowledge base in the past, or if your search uncovers no documents, try your phrase search in a major search engine such as Google.com (see Figure 4.1), which itself serves as an index to online knowledge bases such as Microsoft's. A useful trick here is to restrict your Google search to a particular vendor's site by using the syntax "site:microsoft.com" within your query (replacing "microsoft.com" with the relevant vendor's address). Note further that no search engine indexes the entire Web, and be willing to extend your search with either other general engines or specific tech support sites.

If the knowledge base seems not to hold the answer to your query, you might try repeating it on a site such as FreeAnswers (http://www.freeanswers.com), which indexes the knowledge bases of major vendors and allows you to query in "plain English." If this also fails, check to see if the vendor maintains online discussion forums or an e-mail support group and repeat your search or ask your question there. You can also try asking your question on a relevant library discussion list (see Chapter 5), as your peers in other institutions may have resolved similar issues or have other ideas on where to search. Other options include opening your search up on a major search engine (Google again is a good choice here) to see if a nonvendor Web site has addressed the issue. Here, always be cautious to evaluate the reliability of your source before acting on any advice. Also check your print resources and any documentation to see if your issue is described there.

Remember to avoid relying entirely on one source, whether it's a knowledge base or a favorite manual. Often a source will contain just part of an answer, and putting its clues together with other sources' suggestions and/or your own experience will help you

Figure 4.1   Limiting Google Searches to Specific Tech Sites

find a solution. Some situations will lend themselves to online searching, others to contacting technical support, still others to printed documentation and/or your own maintenance records. As you become a more experienced troubleshooter, you will be able to ascertain more easily the appropriate starting point for your searches and use the knowledge you have gained from resolving related problems to think of solutions to try.

If the affected system is not generating a specific error message you can search for, you will then need to research its behavior. This may take a number of tries before you are able to sort out the correct terminology for your situation. While systems issues fail to come with a set of controlled vocabulary, there are terms and concepts that will be unique to particular products, situations, and vendors. Locating the right terms to search under is a process similar to realizing the necessity of looking in your OPAC under "Cookery—Italian" instead of the straightforward "Italian Cooking." Each profession has its quirks, and the tendency of vendors to try to minimize problems by disguising knowledge base articles under innocuous-sounding headings merely exacerbates this issue.

Our willingness to dig through these various sources until we find an answer, by brute force if necessary, also makes us effective systems librarians. One survey respondent notes: "That second part of that 'reference librarian skill' is the persistence with which one systematically looks for answers, which I think is one of the keys to successful reference librarianship and computer system troubleshooting. If the answer/solution is not in the first, second or third place one looks, one continues to look for a solution/answer in the fourth, fifth, and sixth places. Most often this approach will produce a solution, usually by the third or fourth hypothesis." Like reference librarians, systems librarians cannot afford to give up before an issue is entirely resolved or to settle for the first apparent answer without verifying the information and being willing to dig deeper.

When testing your hypotheses, remember the importance of testing one thing at a time. If one method fails, reverse your steps before applying another fix. If you keep adding potential fix on top of fix, or if you try several solutions simultaneously, you may end up inadvertently creating a larger problem than the one you are trying to resolve. You also create an undocumented situation, in which months later you might be trying to resolve an unrelated issue and not remember that or how you previously changed a specific setting. Always know how to put a system back to its original state, and either do so or keep a record of the changes you have made.

Every time we find a working solution for a technical problem, we add to our existing stores of knowledge and provide ourselves with additional background for later related problems. As in librarianship in general, everything you ever learn about computers will at some point come in handy during your career as a systems librarian. Each support interaction is a potential learning opportunity, and after each you will be better prepared for the troubleshooting activities that follow. While some computer issues may seem truly unique, most occur with some regularity—and if you have kept track of how you previously resolved the same or a similar problem, you will be able to dispatch an issue much more quickly. Terry Ballard's description of the proper state of mind when contemplating troubleshooting issues may be helpful here: "1. The problem can be solved. 2. It is my job to solve it, so the buck stops here. 3. Once it is solved, that will be one more thing that I know how to do."[3] Developing a similar attitude will help you approach your library's technical issues with greater equanimity.

Finally, remember that your librarian-honed research skills are integral to successful troubleshooting. As Lynnette Jack, head of library information technology at the University of Arkansas Little Rock, notes: "The most important aspect of providing good library systems support is the willingness to act as a librarian and find the answer. I am very competent in most areas of systems, but I am not an expert. The greatest asset I bring is good problem solving and tenacity. The answers exist to most problems, you just have to find them."

Dealing with Technical Support

There will inevitably come a time (or hundreds) during your career as an automation librarian when you will need to pry answers out of a company's technical support personnel. Getting to the right piece of information through talking to technical support requires an entire additional level of understanding than does look-ing up answers online or in print. It bears a certain similarity to locating and dealing with the appropriate expert when asked a par-ticularly complicated reference question. You may go through a number of unhelpful individuals before finding your expert, and your expert, once located, might be easily distracted or seem to be speaking some private indecipherable language. But, when you locate the person who is willing and able to resolve your query, the search suddenly becomes worthwhile.

Try not to be reluctant to call tech support because you are less than familiar with their product; they have dealt with plenty of users more novice than you. As IBM site librarian Linda Absher points out: "If you can talk the techie talk, you'll be amazed at how much respect you can garner. Even when I've had to fake it, it's given credibility when dealing with tech support." As in many other aspects of systems librarianship, a familiarity with the basic concepts and facility for clear communication (in explaining what you have already tried and the specific behavior the system is exhibiting) will stand you in good stead when dealing with support personnel.

Calling or e-mailing tech support will often be your last resort when information cannot be located through other sources. It is also an option when you suspect that a quick and simple solution exists, and that contacting support directly will allow you to resolve a situation in the most expeditious manner. Before dialing or writing, however, realize that most front-line technical support personnel are used to dealing primarily with computer novices. Be patient when asked if your computer is plugged in, your monitor is turned on, and any of the other basic and seemingly insulting questions that come with dealing with this level. (And, remember to think of asking such basic questions when trying to resolve issues on your own; do not assume that a problem always has a complicated answer!) If you get an automated or irrelevant response to your first e-mail, answer with additional details—or pick up the phone. Persevere with patience, and your (likely more complicated) issue will eventually be escalated up to someone who can help. More knowledgeable personnel will not be answering phones on the front lines, because their time would be wasted by having to focus on the preponderance of calls dealing with easily resolvable issues.

When dealing with technical support, also document your issue as extensively as possible. If your system is giving an error, for example, technical support will need to know exactly what that error message is; write it down! Have you dealt with technical support before on the same (or a similar) issue? Have it documented—and get the names of representatives you deal with, and incident numbers, if applicable. (See Chapter 3 for more on the importance of keeping thorough documentation.)

Your institution may also wish to invest in a cell phone or portable phone for your use while dealing with tech support, so that you can call while near PCs that lack accessible phone lines. Remember, however, that concentrations of computer equipment can interfere with the reception of both, and that 2.4G portables may disrupt nearby 8.0211b wireless networks, which use the same spectrum.

Another support option in many instances is to look for answers (or post your question) on a vendor's technical support online forum or e-mail discussion list. (See more on networking online in the Chapter 5.) A number of companies host online forums on their support sites, which are optimally staffed by technical support personnel. You can browse through previously asked questions to see if other users have encountered a similar issue, or ask your own question of the support rep monitoring that forum. An added bonus is that you may often find your question answered by another user who has encountered the same problem and is willing to take the time to explain how it was resolved.

Lastly, find out what technical support options are available from your larger institution, system, or consortium. If your system headquarters or campus computing center, for example, employs a networking expert whose responsibilities include resolving network issues among member libraries, contact that individual first if a LAN problem looks too difficult or time-consuming for you to resolve on the local end. Be sure to contact them first if your issue seems to affect the system rather than just your institution, or if it affects equipment they have provided or software they have installed. Develop a relationship with the systems staff there so that you are able to draw upon their expertise when needed and so that you are less likely to be left out of the loop when it is time to make systemwide decisions that will affect your local network and/or computing environment. Find out which types of issues are appropriate to escalate, and refrain from referring every minor problem, but know when it is necessary to call on your larger institution for help. Also find out whom to contact at your larger institution when you need them to make changes that affect your local network, for example, if you need additions made to your proxy server or changes made to your filtering software in cases where these are hosted at the system end.

Always escalate an issue to your larger institution, if possible, before paying for technical support from a vendor. If you are faced with making the decision as to when to contact pay-for-support, a good rough guideline is to estimate the number of hours you have spent—or seem likely to spend—resolving the problem in-house. What is your (or your staff's) time worth to your library? Multiply the number of hours you spend on a problem by your hourly salary, and, if you are spending more by keeping the work in-house than you would on the support call, you are not really saving your institution any money. While you are tied up resolving one issue, other tasks may go undone. Do realize that many pay-for-support options will require a credit card number, which libraries tend to dole out sparingly. Be prepared to explain your need to the appropriate manager or business office employee.

The Support Interview

Systems librarians are generally in the position of both having to deal with outside technical support and serving as help desk or technical support in their own institution. Again, you will tend to find yourself in the role of liaison, translating vendor-speak, contacting tech support for an affected user, and identifying the real problem behind a given user's request.

Any librarian who has been through introductory reference coursework—or who has worked at a public services desk—is familiar with the concept of the reference interview. Your background in ferreting out the real question behind an initial encounter will come in handy when a staff member or library patron begins a technical support interaction with: "This computer isn't working!" Now it is your turn to be on the other side of that tech support call. Viewing your technical support encounter as a reference interview will also help you view this process as a collaborative effort between yourself and the affected patron or staff member. Your main goal in a support encounter will be to resolve the problem to the user's satisfaction, but your secondary goals can include identifying the real issue, identifying whether there are related or underlying issues that might also need resolving, and identifying opportunities to use the encounter as a learning opportunity. (These aspects are, of course, ideal, and in a busy library environment you may often be satisfied with just getting a user up and running again.)

The first step in your technical support interview will be to get a detailed description of the problem. Start from: "This computer isn't working!" and ask targeted questions to ascertain the real issue. Useful questions to help narrow down the exact problem include: "What exactly is it doing?" "Is it displaying an error message?" "What were you doing when the problem occurred?" and so on. If this is a recurring glitch, try to have your staff members or patrons recreate the issue. Have them show you exactly what they are doing when the situation occurs. Try to get specific error messages out of them; identify the specific software and version they are using; find out when the problem started; see if they have installed software or otherwise modified their machine without your knowledge; see if the machine has been experiencing minor problems for a long time, which now have escalated to the point where the user cannot function.

It will often be easier to observe an individual's actual workflow than to have her try to explain her exact sequence of actions when a problem occurs. As one survey respondent notes: "The most important skill is probably not computer based at all. It is the ability to do troubleshooting based on symptoms of a problem. A good example is that recently records on the catalog were getting overlaid on a regular basis with old information that had been changed. It took several weeks to figure out the problem but I finally observed our cataloger's detailed workflow. She was forgetting to purge or delete old files."

If you are in a larger institution and feel confident in your ability to train your coworkers to report problems accurately, or if there are often times when no systems staff is available to resolve technical issues, you may wish to develop a standardized method of reporting computer problems. Create a printed fill-in-the-blank form that can be kept at central locations such as the reference and circulation desks, and use this form to coax usable information out of the reporting staff member. Include space for the date, the location of the affected machine (here your inventory numbering system will be useful in easily identifying which system needs work), the name of the staff member, any error messages generated, a description of the issue, and anything the staff member may have done (reboot, change settings) to try to resolve the problem on her own. Many computer repair shops use a similar form to describe problems when items are dropped off for repair; you may be able to borrow ideas from your local vendor and adapt the format for use in your library.

Some libraries find it useful to use the back of their standard "Out of Service" signs for these reports, so that the person putting a piece of equipment out of order is also responsible for filling out the form. Others prefer that forms be given directly to the systems librarian or support department so that the situation can be dealt with as quickly as possible. Make sure that all staff know to whom they should report computer outages. If you have several systems personnel, make it clear whether staff should report problems to different individuals or whether you prefer centralized reporting. Remember also that it is often more difficult for users to describe a problem in writing than in person, and take the time to speak directly with the reporting staff member before attempting to resolve the situation if the written report seems unclear or incomplete.

Sample Computer Problem Report

Date: Reported By:

Inventory Number: Item Location:

Please describe the problem, in as much detail as possible:

List any specific error messages the system is generating:

List any steps you have already taken to try to resolve this issue:

You can keep these forms on file to help you identify machines that constantly act up. You might also wish to create a maintenance reporting form for yourself and/or your systems staff that gives the date and resolution of each of these issues. This completed form can then be kept on file with your inventory or in each system's motherboard box so that you have both a record of what has been done and a reference to consult if the issue occurs again in the future.

Try to create an environment in which library staff feel comfortable approaching you and/or your staff with their computer problems. While many staff members might seem to approach you with every minor issue, others will not want to "waste your time" or may feel they are exposing their technological ignorance by asking for help. If not dealt with, however, minor issues tend to evolve into major ones. Users who have become frustrated by constant minor annoyances will tend to be less comfortable with technology and more resistant to change. This is another reason why people skills are so important. Always ensure that staff members understand that these problems lie with the computer, not with them, and that you want them to come to your department with even seemingly minor issues.

Back up this request with a willingness to deal with such issues as swiftly as possible. This response requires developing the ability to prioritize your time and to differentiate actual issues from minor glitches that may just require a reboot. (See more on teaching staff to do minor troubleshooting and identify real problems in Chapter 9.) Make sure that if you have several systems people on site, all staff members know who they can go to with their computer problems. If one systems person, for example, is in charge of networking and one is a printer whiz, make this information accessible to all staff so that the right person can resolve a given issue as swiftly as possible. (If you are a one-person shop, then, of course, all queries will come directly to you!)

You may need at first to be more proactive; set a regular time to go around the building and talk to staff about their computing environment, their needs, and their issues. Those who will not come to you directly might be willing to share their frustrations if you show your openness by first coming to them. While making your rounds, take the opportunity to engage in some preventative maintenance; bring some canned air and clean out case fans, defragment hard drives, and open up mice and dislodge dust and lint. While it might be difficult to fit proactive maintenance into your schedule, setting aside a couple of hours each week will help prevent larger and more time-consuming problems in the future, as well as help you become acquainted with other library staff members and their specific needs.

Researching Technology Purchases

Any savvy consumer knows the importance of researching major purchases before investing. This is doubly important when you are dealing with your institution's somewhat larger budget and recommending and approving the purchase of software, products, and services on which your staff and users must rely—and which you are responsible for maintaining. Researching and speccing out technology purchases and getting competitive quotes from vendors will also be necessary in many public and academic libraries, especially when a purchase will be funded with grant or other specially acquired funding. It will be easier to recommend technology purchases if you develop the habit of keeping yourself continually informed about recent technological developments and possibilities. (See more on this in Chapter 7.) If you know your institution will be in the market for a particular technology solution in the foreseeable future, remain alert for articles on and mentions of that technology in your daily reading.

Also, develop a collection of resources you can consult when researching such purchases. These resources can include Web sites, discussion lists and list archives, colleagues in other institutions, journal articles, product reviews, and so on. Outside sources and those who have used a particular product or service can help you evaluate its merits before committing to its purchase. Recommendations from your peers on software purchases can be especially useful, as the library environment presents special challenges for the smooth running and deployment of many programs. Your colleagues may be able to alert you to problems with particular packages in a public-access environment, or to any adverse interactions between popular security software and the products you are evaluating.

As in systems librarianship in general, your previous experiences and your network of resources provide the foundation for evaluating potential purchases in terms of your library's needs. Your past experiences with the time taken and aggravation created by having to maintain and troubleshoot generic, lower-priced PCs, for example, may lead you to investigate name-brand replacements in the future—even if the initial cost may seem higher. Your experience with machines that were not easily upgradeable may lead you to ask questions about expansion slots and case design. Your experience with poorly designed navigation and search schemes may lead you to request trial access to an online database and allow public services staff to experiment with its usability before committing to its purchase. When evaluating any technology purchase, consider the total cost of ownership, which includes the time taken by staff in maintaining, learning, and effectively using the product. This is doubly important if you are a solo systems librarian, as your time could be better spent than in repeatedly troubleshooting the same off-brand or poorly designed systems.

When evaluating these purchases, investigate both the reliability of a given vendor and its reputation for providing technical support. If you have limited support from your larger institution and/or no other systems staff in your library, you will need to rely on support from your outside vendors. Again, watch systems librarian lists for comments on specific vendors, read compara- tive articles in computer journals, and ask others about their sup- port experiences. If you read nightmare stories about others' support interactions with a given vendor, you might reconsider purchasing that vendor's product. Even if that product initially seems the most cost-effective solution for your institution, it may in the long run end up costing you more in terms of your time and your users' lost productivity. Try to look at the big picture and not only a single issue, such as price or initial convenience. Also pay attention to warranty periods on hardware (which should be at least one year) and ascertain whether support is included in the initial pricing, or whether on-site or telephone support is pro- vided only for an additional cost.

When evaluating software and database purchases, be alert to offers of free demo software, on-site vendor demos, and other opportunities to try before you buy so that you can better see if a particular piece of software will meet your institution's needs. Demos may also let you see how the software will work in your environment, under your security software, and with the other programs on your network before you commit to a purchase. Always ask for trial access to online databases and other electronic resources; never commit to purchasing an expensive electronic database without having an opportunity to evaluate the product in your own institution. Here, resources such as *Library Journal's* Free Trial Zone (http://freetrialzone.com) may be useful in identifying options and setting up trials, especially as more vendors sign on to the concept. Otherwise, peruse vendor Web sites for trial offers or contact an individual vendor's sales department to see what options you have. Look for reviews of electronic resources and online databases to help you evaluate products before purchasing, since many library review journals now include coverage of these products in their review sections.

Researching purchases also involves researching different departments' technological needs. If you have kept the lines of communication open between yourself and nonsystems staff, you will have a better idea of the library's true needs. Involving other departments, especially in the purchase of electronic resources that they may be using on a daily basis, also helps avoid the impression that decisions are coming from on high with no opportunity for staff input. While you will provide the technical expertise behind a purchase decision, involving others is essential in making sure that these purchases serve the needs of your institution.

It may help to approach researching technology purchases as you would approach researching any large collection development purchase. You can apply similar criteria as to cost, suitability for your library's population, timeliness, and so on—and use review sources to help you make a decision just as you would in researching the purchase of, say, a major art encyclopedia. Also evaluate products and services in terms of your current computing environment and what you have previously purchased, just as you would when adding to the rest of your collection.

If you work in an academic, public, or school library, realize that your institution is also eligible for academic or government discounts on most software and some hardware purchases. Sometimes these discounts can be substantial, and will allow your library to purchase packages and equipment it could never otherwise afford. Always investigate academic/governmental pricing options, whether from the vendor itself or from approved resellers such as CDW's and Dell's governmental divisions. Some software is even free for nonprofit and/or academic use—check the license agreements of your shareware programs for such clauses. (Ipswitch's popular WS_FTP LE graphical FTP software is an example of one such program.)

Another factor to researching purchases is the process of deciding when and whether technology purchases, especially replacements of existing hardware and software, actually become necessary. While old equipment, for example, may still function perfectly well for the purpose for which it was originally purchased, you need to ask a number of questions to find out whether it is time to upgrade. These questions include: Do users need new software for compatibility purposes or because you are upgrading the ILS or otherwise changing the computing atmosphere? Can your older hardware handle the newer software you are installing? Can older hardware be upgraded or repurposed? Is it cost-effective to do so? Does newer software offer features that will be useful to staff or patrons, or are they spending enough time working around issues created by the use of older programs that it is affecting productivity? Have vendors ceased supporting the older hardware or software? What funding is available for upgrades, and can alternative sources be found? Is older hardware requiring constant maintenance?

The answers to these questions will help you determine the appropriate replacement cycle. Be sure to look at overall costs of using older equipment and programs, including reduced productivity of staff and users as well as your and your department's time. Your inventory and maintenance records will be useful here in determining the existing state of computing equipment and answers to some of these questions, and knowing your department's level of funding will help you determine whether you can realistically keep to an ideal replacement cycle or whether you will need to seek out alternative sources of revenue.

Overall, knowing where and how to look for an answer will be one of the most important building blocks in your successful systems librarian career. Take time to develop the research and critical thinking skills necessary for resolving the issues that will inevitably arise.

Works Cited

1. Burke, John J. *Neal-Schuman Library Technology Companion.* New York: Neal-Schuman, 2001: 17.

2. Bates, Mary Ellen. "The Newly Minted MLS: What Do We Need To Know Today?" *Searcher,* May 1998. 30 April 2002 (http://www.infotoday.com/searcher/may98/story1.htm).

3. Ballard, Terry. "Zen in the Art of Troubleshooting." *American Libraries,* January 1994: 108.

Chapter 5

Networking

> *"The commiserating of fellow soldiers in the computing wars is a salve beyond belief. All people employed in these activities have faced similar affronts to their technical ability, personal integrity, and mental sanity."*
> —Thomas C. Wilson[1]

Successful automation librarians know that networking extends far beyond deciding where to drop the Ethernet cable. One of the most important factors in our ongoing achievement is the array of professional and social networks we foster among our peers, our vendors, and our colleagues. While we are able to use the skills honed in our Research Techniques lessons to find answers to many problems independently, the best source of support will often be a colleague or other professional who has already been there. Interacting with other systems people can also give us ideas for ways to improve the technological environment in our own institutions and to reduce our own workloads, as well as provide answers to questions we may not even have thought to ask. Lastly, networking with other systems professionals allows us to understand that we are not alone, and that there are others sharing similar frustrations, stresses—and successes. Both formal and informal networking groups provide the opportunity for brainstorming, resource sharing, and seeing examples of what other libraries are doing and can do with technology.

Systems librarians can find a number of opportunities to interact with others in similar situations, both on- and offline. In the following pages, you will find recommendations on effectively interacting through and locating online discussion groups and in-person technology interest groups and associations, as well as cultivating informal support networks with peers, staff, and colleagues. Each of these networking methods is essential to your success (and sanity); there is no single way to connect with other systems librarians. As survey respondent Karen Knox, head of systems and technology at Novi Public Library, advises: "Collaborate with other library technology folks. ... Together, we do much more than we could do on our own. And if there's something that I am not familiar with, chances are someone else at another library is. This way, the library technology world is much more manageable!"

Online Discussion Groups

As you might expect, there are a number of online forums where library systems workers can interact and share their knowledge. Online e-mail lists and other discussion forums have the advantage of leveling the field; systems staff in the smallest, most under-funded library are equally as able to participate in these conversations as those in larger institutions with the funding to attend costly in-person conferences and workshops. Lists provide a venue for discussion with colleagues even when no other systems personnel are handy to consult within our own institution. Lists can provide a place for quick feedback on your systems questions; further, the ability to post a technical question or comment and then return at your leisure for a response will help you fit participation into your schedule. They provide a source for keeping apprised of virus and security alerts on common library applications, which can allow you to forestall technical problems in your own institution. Beyond troubleshooting assistance, systems lists also provide the opportunity to discuss broader issues facing systems librarians and a source of community for those, especially solo systems librarians, who otherwise may have a tendency to get bogged down in day-to-day technical tasks.

Selected Online Discussion Groups for Systems Librarians

- *DIG_REF*: http://www.vrd.org/Dig_Ref/dig_ref.shtml. Explores digital reference services in libraries.

- *DIGLIB*: http://www.ifla.org/II/lists/diglib.htm. For discussion of digitization in libraries.

- *Electronic Resources in Libraries*: http://www.topica.com/lists/eril. Deals with the selection and management of electronic resources in libraries; covers issues such as collection development, statistics, and licensing.

- *LIBNT-L*: http://listserv.utk.edu/archives/libnt-l.html. Discussions center around the use and management of Windows NT (and now Windows 2000/XP) in libraries.

- *Libsoft:* http://www.orst.edu/groups/libsoft. For discussion of useful software for libraries.

- *LibWireless:* To subscribe, e-mail a blank message to lib-wireless-subscribe@ls.suny.edu. For discussion of wireless technologies in a library setting.

- *Linux-in-libraries*: http://apocalypse.unomaha.edu/lil. Discussions on using Linux in a library environment.

- *LITA-L*: http://www.lita.org/lists.htm. Announcements and discussion relating to LITA's (Library Information and Technology Association) interests.

- *NETTRAIN*: http://listserv.acsu.buffalo.edu/archives/nettrain.html. An e-mail discussion list for Internet and computer trainers, not specifically focused on libraries.

- *oss4lib-discuss*: http://lists.sourceforge.net/listslistinfo/oss4lib-discuss. A companion e-mail list to the oss4lib Weblog (http://www.oss4lib.org), which covers the use of open source software in libraries. Often contains links to useful free utilities written or recommended by list members.

- *PACS-L*: http://info.lib.uh.edu/pacsl.html. Discuss end-user computer systems in libraries, including OPACs and electronic databases.

- *Perl4Lib:* http://www.rice.edu/perl4lib. For exchange of programs and ideas from Perl programmers in libraries.

- *Public Library Computer Trainers:* http://www.topica.com/lists/publibct. Share notes and tips on teaching computer skills in a public library setting.

- *SYSLIB-L*: http://listserv.acsu.buffalo.edu/archives/syslib-l.html. The major e-mail list for systems librarians, covering all aspects of systems work in libraries. A great place to ask questions; start by searching the list's archives to see if others have encountered similar situations.

- *Web4Lib*: http://sunsite.berkeley.edu/Web4Lib. For library Web managers. Talk about Web design issues, managing public Internet access, and training staff and users to use the Web and/or Web resources. Its online archives are a great resource for designers and for those managing servers and sites at their libraries.

- *XML4Lib:* http://sunsite.berkeley.edu/XML4Lib. On the use of XML in the library environment.

See the sidebar for suggestions on systems lists to join. Find additional groups at Library-Oriented Lists and Electronic Serials (http://liblists.wrlc.org/home.htm) or ask colleagues to recommend groups that they find helpful. Also, do not limit yourself entirely to lists for systems librarians; lists for IT professionals, technology trainers, and Web designers may be just as useful to you. For more general lists, try searching by subject on Topica (http://www.topica.com), PAML (Publicly Accessible Mailing Lists, http://paml.net) and CataList (http://www.lsoft.com/catalist.html). If your ILS vendor offers a list (or lists), consider joining, or at least ensure that someone on your system staff or at the consortial level follows the discussions and forwards pertinent information. Your larger system or consortium may also have a list to support a technical task force or user group, as may national library associations and their subgroups.

Successful online interaction requires attention to just a few simple ground rules. When you first join an online discussion group, read any introductory messages (and the FAQ, if available) carefully. These messages will provide you with the scope of appropriate discussion on the particular list or forum, and adherence to the guidelines will prevent you from asking off-topic questions or making comments that might be more appropriate in another venue. The guidelines will also provide instructions for leaving the group at a later date. (Never, ever post repeatedly to an online group—especially a systems group—asking how to unsubscribe; you will succeed merely in annoying its members.) Before making your first post, read some previous discussions, and, if asking for help, check the group's online archives to see if your question has already been answered. The rest is common sense: treat other group members with professional courtesy and respect and lend your own expertise if you are able to answer a question posed by another member. Remember that at least some systems people have been online longer, possess more expertise, and have likely exhausted their tolerance for breaches of netiquette; participate appropriately.

Managing your time online requires mastery of the grand art of skimming; read and file what is appropriate for your situation and ignore (or delete) the rest. Do not feel compelled to read every message that comes through every list. No one will know! If the traffic on a particular list gets to be too much for you, unsubscribe. You can always schedule periodic trips to its online archives to pull out any relevant material you may have missed. (Also, if you do make a habit of skimming, be sure to read recent archives before posting to ensure that you are not repeating a point someone else has just made.)

Lists provide the perfect opportunity for learning from other technology librarians' experiences. The pool of discussion group participants is large enough that it is likely that others have resolved similar problems or worked in similar situations. Group members' willingness to share these experiences and their expertise creates a true online community of experts, and no systems librarian can afford to remain outside this community. Once you have made online contact with group members, you may strike up an "off-list" conversation and develop a more personal relationship with group members in similar situations. Beyond providing a forum for group discussions, e-mail is also exceedingly useful for one-on-one communication. Building a personal contact list of experts will give you a community to call upon for technical and personal support, and you may in this way also locate potential mentors in other institutions.

This pool of colleagues and experts is especially useful to an accidental systems librarian who lacks a ready source of technical support in her own institution. It is easy to feel professionally isolated when you are the only systems person in your institution, and online participation can help reduce those feelings. As you can see from the sidebar, there are lists focusing on nearly every topic of interest to library systems personnel; systems librarians in all types of libraries appreciate the support and collegiality these groups provide. Many systems questions particularly lend themselves to being answered via e-mail, as group members can easily point to online resources and examples. Further, groups allow you to ask questions on newer or more library-specific issues that may not be retrievable from an easily accessible print or online resource.

Beyond e-mail lists, Web-based support forums and systems discussion groups provide another opportunity for learning and for building community. While most of these are not specifically focused on the library environment, they will still prove useful to technology librarians in all sorts of situations. See, for example, the online forums at SysAds.org (http://www.sysads.org), which include discussion topics such as Windows NT/2000 systems administration and Linux administration. Take the opportunity online resources provide to broaden your scope and to interact with systems peers in other environments.(See Figure 5.1.)

Interest Groups

While online discussion groups present an invaluable networking opportunity, especially for busy professionals whose duties allow little time for in-person communication, there are also times

Figure 5.1   Online Forums at SysAds.org

when more old-fashioned networking is necessary—if only for the opportunity for getting out from behind the computer screen. Technology interest groups (sometimes called committees, user groups, special interest groups, or forums) provide a built-in forum for networking, and members who meet in this way can then keep in touch between in-person meetings through the use of e-mail and other online tools.

An Interview with ILA RSTF
Technology User Group Co-Chair
Lori Bell (January 2002)

Could you briefly describe your technology interest group, its purpose, number of members, and regular activities? When was the group established, and what prompted its formation?

I will answer these two questions at once. ... The Illinois Library Association Resources and Technical Services Forum Technology User Group was formed in November 2001. A small group initially proposed a technology forum to the ILA Board in 2000, but were asked to first become part of an existing forum. In the past, forums had been formed and then were folded due to lack of interest or leadership. Rather than starting a new forum, the technology user group became a group under RTSF.

The purpose of the technology user group is to provide ILA members from libraries of all types with a networking group for technology ideas, news, applications, and training opportunities in the area of library technology. Currently, there are almost 50 people signed up for the electronic mailing list. The first meeting was held at Eureka College November 28, and had approximately 25 people attending.

The group plans to meet quarterly in different areas of the state with each meeting featuring a technology program, and a discussion of technology trends in libraries. The group is loosely based upon the ALA LITA Top Tech Trends Committee. The other co-chair of the group, Tom Peters, is a member of this group and will report at each meeting on the top tech trends committee. The group has also proposed a number of technology programs for the ILA Conference.

How do members communicate between meetings? Can you give some examples of topics that have been discussed/ shared?

Between meetings, the group communicates on the electronic mailing list. Some of the examples of topics in the brief time since formation have included Weblogs, technology trends for 2002, Web portals, open source software, ILA program ideas, and so on.

What types of programs does the ILA RTSF Technology Users Group plan to offer in the future?

In February, our meeting is on Web portals/bloggers and accidental systems librarianship. ... Our next meeting will be in June—two of the libraries/librarians involved in the group received a grant, so they are holding a continuing education on PDAs event. The next meeting will be in the Chicago area at a public library with a community network and a high tech training lab and the discussion will be on using community partnerships to leverage technology. The ILA Conference follows that.

Your group's Weblog (http://www.techusers.blogspot.com) is an interesting collaborative exercise. How did the log begin, and what kind of participation have you seen so far? Do you limit its use to group members?

The log began because of an idea Teri Ross Embrey from Chicago Library System had. The group discussed an idea to promote innovative technology projects in Illinois as a Web portal and Teri suggested we try a Weblog. So far, there are about 10 people participating and its use is not limited to group members.

What benefits do you see accruing to group members?

The group has a great diversity in that there are members from all types of libraries. This provides for a rich and unique sharing of ideas across library types. People can share expertise, meet others with the same interests across the state, and gain knowledge about new technologies they can apply in their library.

> *Is there anything else you'd like to share about the group that has not been covered here?*
>
> I hope the group will meet a need and be successful!

Interest groups may be subgroups of larger more general associations, or they may be more informal networking groups formed by like-minded information professionals. If you are in a large library system or city, you may be able to join a local technology group, but most systems librarians should begin searching for relevant technology interest groups at the level of their state library association. (See more on association involvement in the next section.) Joining a technology interest group in your state provides in-person networking opportunities with nearby systems personnel. You may also be more likely to gain institutional funding and/or administrative backing to attend local meetings with such groups than with those of national organizations, which will generally require travel. If your system, area, or state association lacks a technology interest group, consider starting one. Rest assured that there will be a number of systems librarians eager to attend and to share their expertise.

The Illinois Library Association's RTSF Technology User's Group (see interview in sidebar) serves as an example of such a local networking group. Most members are able to attend at least some of the group's regular meetings, which are held in different locations around the state to attract nearby systems personnel. This in-person contact adds another dimension to the group's online discussion list and Weblog, as most members know each other from having met at conferences, meetings, and workshops. In-person meetings add a level of understanding of each other's circumstances that can be more difficult to achieve in a purely online environment.

Also consider joining a technology interest subgroup of a larger, national association. Examples of these smaller subgroups include LITA's Heads of Library Technology or Open Source Systems interest groups. (Note, however, that, as with other divisions and roundtables, ALA membership is currently required before you can join LITA. This imposes a double dues burden, as you end up paying for both groups. See if your library will pick up the tab for membership in one or both organizations.)

While you will likely be unable to meet in-person with your colleagues as often as you might in a state or local group, you will be able to broaden the scope of your involvement and interact with other professionals nationwide. Especially if you are able regularly to attend ALA Annual or other national conferences during which these groups hold their meetings, smaller roundtables or interest groups provide a useful networking opportunity. Consider volunteering for the leadership of such groups or to participate in subcommittees in which you have an interest. Most are actively seeking volunteers, and your institution might also be more likely to financially support your attendance at meetings if you can demonstrate your active involvement.

You may also consider joining local nonlibrary technology user groups, especially if you want to shore up or share your skills in a particular area. These user groups may not be as useful as groups for librarians, however, because members are not coming from the same background and will have different perspectives on how technology should be deployed.

Associations and Conferences

There are a number of national associations targeted to the needs of library systems staff. Chief among these are LITA and the American Society for Information Science and Technology (ASIST). Although it can be more difficult to attend in-person meetings of such groups, given the cost of conference fees, travel, and hotels, some associations are trying to bridge the gap by providing electronic archiving of conference presentations. (For an example of this, see ASIST's 2001 annual conference page at http://www.asis.org/digiscript.html. Note that purchase is required for nonattendees.) Associations such as LITA, furthermore, are working to broaden their reach and educate others through holding "Regional Institutes"—one-day workshops held in different locations around the country, focusing on specific technology topics in libraries (recent topics include e-books, database-driven Web sites, and proxy servers). LITA also considers proposals for additional institutes or requests to develop an institute on a particular topic; see http://www.lita.org/institut. Regional Institutes and related programs allow you to pursue continuing education opportunities through your association beyond its annual conference.

As an association member, you will also be entitled to receive publications of the association, such as LITA's *Information Technology and Libraries* quarterly journal (a refereed publication focusing on all aspects of libraries and information technology) and ASIST's *Journal of ASIST*. Such publications often contain articles of use to working systems librarians and can serve as a content awareness tool. Other benefits that accrue to association members include the ability to join online discussion forums (which may be members-only) and interact with fellow members between conferences, reduced conference fees, and the opportunity to participate in decision making.

If you are fortunate enough to be able to attend out-of-state annual meetings, each of these associations provides useful in-person networking and learning opportunities. ASIST, for example, holds an annual conference, a mid-year conference, and an annual summit on information architecture, and conference fees are heavily discounted for association members. LITA offers an annual national forum, and, since it is a division of ALA, also holds meetings at ALA Midwinter and Annual Conferences. This can be a useful way to combine your technical and general conference attendance and to network with systems colleagues while also attending less targeted programs and meetings. Also look for pre-conference offerings, which can provide opportunities to attend longer and more focused seminars on major topics such as open source software.

Keep alert also to opportunities for informal networking at such conferences during lunch breaks, talk tables, and encounters at exhibitors' booths. Make e-mail appointments to meet with your virtual colleagues at such events. Take time to approach a speaker you find particularly interesting after a presentation has concluded, or e-mail her after the convention with a question or comment on her talk. Conferences can be a useful job-hunting tool, as well; for more on this, see Chapter 9.

While evaluating whether to attend your association's conferences, also consider attending one or more of the major technology-related conferences for librarians that are not linked to a particular association. Premiere among these is the annual Computers in Libraries conference, which generally includes sessions on a number of topics relevant to systems librarianship. A sampling of topics for 2002 includes e-books, XML for librarians, Web site usability, digital reference services, securing public access on modern OPACs, wireless networks, and PDAs. Because such conferences are not tied to the agenda of any particular group and do not have to compete for space with general sessions as at conferences such as ALA Annual and Midwinter, all of the sessions and workshops can concentrate on practical, hands-on topics for systems librarians. Also keep an eye out for relevant library symposia on topics such as building digital collections and virtual reference service and for related conferences on technology, knowledge management, and digital information; these are often announced on topical e-mail lists for systems librarians.

Another networking opportunity presents itself in the form of your ILS user group meetings. What better common ground than running the same automation system, which means you will be encountering many of the same issues. The sessions at user group meetings also give a number of ideas for extending the functionality of your system, for training, and so on, and these ideas provide a number of conversational starting points.

You might yourself consider presenting at one of these association meetings or computer-related conferences. If your library has found an interesting use for technology or if you have resolved a common problem, why not share your knowledge with your colleagues? You can start small by volunteering to lead a talk table or serve on a panel at your state conference, which will help you build your confidence in front of a smaller group before presenting at a national meeting. Presenting provides additional networking opportunities, as well as the chance to add to your resume and demonstrate your speaking skills to future employers. Keep alert to calls for papers and presenters on e-mail discussion lists and in the print literature; these provide the opportunity for you to describe and test your theories and thoughts in interaction with a live audience.

Lastly, while at any conference, do not neglect to take the time to check out the vendor exhibits. This can be a great way to gain information on new and forthcoming products, talk to vendor representatives to get in-person insights, sign up for demos, and see in-person demonstrations of both hardware and software products. It may be easier to try a product out with a representative present to answer any on-the-spot questions you have, and an exhibit hall also provides the perfect opportunity to compare several competing technologies side-by-side. You can generally find a list of exhibitors in preconference information provided online or in an association journal; use this to plan visits to specific vendors whose products interest you. Be mindful, however, that vendor demos at a conference may be somewhat misleading as to a product's actual performance in a real-world environment. Demos may work from a smaller database (with correspondingly fast retrieval times) or on customized or expensive equipment, under very controlled circumstances. Ask tough questions, and demo a product at your home institution, if possible, before purchasing.

Informal Networks

While formal associations and other technology-related groups have their place, the informal networks you create with other systems librarians, IT personnel, library staff, and colleagues in other libraries are also essential building blocks in your networking edifice. When asked what one piece of advice they would give to an aspiring library automation specialist, many survey respondents mentioned the importance of building these relationships. Typical comments included:

- "I'd tell them to develop a good rapport with their automation vendor's tech support people and, most importantly, with the folks on their staff. Staff members can kill you."

- "Develop and nurture your listening skills—you must be able to hear and comprehend the perspective of your staff and patrons!"

- "Don't work in a vacuum. Stay in touch with who is using the system."

- "Learn how to interact with your peers and patrons as well as you do with your computers."

- "You will not be alone, so ask for help."

- "Use communication networks freely. Library staff are always willing to share ideas and help if possible."

- "Network!"

Working with technology can have the unfortunate side effect of isolating you from fellow staff members and colleagues. It is easy to develop a tendency to spend more time going one-on-one with the computer screen than communicating with others, and it may seem that your nonsystems coworkers lack a common basis for understanding your positions and workload. Be on the alert for this, and recognize the importance of promoting communication among all of these groups.

Consciously networking with other staff members in your institution, especially non-IT staff, helps keep you connected both to your coworkers and to larger institutional objectives. When working in IT, it is easy to become narrowly focused on the day-to-day tasks of keeping computer technology up and running; while interacting with other librarians can help you re-ground yourself in the foundations of librarianship. You and your coworkers do share common goals, and if technology is not helping your coworkers meet these goals (or if it seems to frustrate their achievement of them!), you need to be aware. Make sure that you are approachable and that you are also open to talking about non-computer-related topics. Often staff will not even know the questions to ask, or what might be possible, so talking with them about their overall wishes and needs allows you to show them how (or think of ways) technology might be able to meet those needs.

When you neglect the cultivation of your informal network with other librarians in your institution, you thwart the goal of serving as a liaison between IT personnel and others in your institution. Remember from Chapter 1 this integral role of systems librarians who serve to bridge the gap between what is sometimes perceived as two completely different worlds. This gap can be exacerbated if your only contact with staff is in a tech support role. You may work in systems, but you are still, and foremost, a librarian. Colleagues with an interest in technology, further, can be valuable allies in smaller libraries where you do not have an official IT staff or systems department to assist you. Power users and tinkerers who have been there since a system was installed will often possess pockets of knowledge that you should not neglect to mine.

Beyond networking with library staff in your own institution, do not neglect your network of peers in neighboring libraries. Other systems librarians in your library system or consortium likely face very similar issues; they may use the same automation system, do group buys of electronic resources and/or computer hardware, and/or belong to the same WAN. Because of these commonalities, these peers are often your best resource for both systems advice and commiseration.

Developing Networking Skills

It is easy to become isolated after graduating from library school, especially if you move out-of-state to take a position or find yourself in a smaller library with a limited pool of peers. Systems librarians can find themselves more isolated by the very nature of their work—it can be difficult for nonsystems people to understand your day-to-day struggles with technology, and much of your work will be done independently. These factors, however, make it all the more important to try to actively develop your networking skills and reach out to your colleagues both on the technical and nontechnical sides.

Here it can be helpful to learn from your connected peers. If you know another librarian who seems to know someone at any institution and who always has a wide network of colleagues to call upon, take note of how she builds these relationships. As Mary Heiberger observes: "It may also be helpful to watch people who seem to have wide networks. What do they seem to do? How do they act at conferences? How do they act at departmental collo- quia? What do you see them doing that you might want to emu- late? Realize that behaviors that now look easy are habits that these people also had to work to develop."[2] Go to a conference with oth- ers from your institution, or meet up with people you have talked to on mailing lists. Ask the colleagues you do know to take some time to introduce you to their peers in other libraries. Ask intelli- gent questions about what they are doing at their institutions, and share your work with them.

Note that networking implies a two-way process. Always be will- ing to serve as a resource for your colleagues just as you wish oth- ers to be a resource for you. Contribute your expertise and findings as appropriate on mailing lists and in both formal and informal discussions with your peers. Remember that you are part of the "invisible college" of systems librarians; both contributing to and drawing from a joint pool of expertise and experience.

Collaboration

Beyond networking for professional development purposes or to solve immediate issues, you might also find yourself collaborat- ing with colleagues in other institutions or other departments within your own institution on certain large-scale projects. For example, you might need to work closely with your counterpart in another institution or library system to set up Z39.50 access to each other's online catalogs. You may work with a distance-learning unit in your university to create Web sites that provide access to library- supported electronic resources. You may work with the systems department in your larger institution to track down a networking issue affecting your interconnected systems. You may cooperate with other institutions in selecting and sharing licensing costs for online databases—cooperation within a consortium can result in

122 The Accidental Systems Librarian

significant savings. You may collaborate with other libraries and historical societies in joint digitization projects. Even if you are a solo systems librarian in your own institution, in many cases, you will not always be working in isolation.

The necessity for cooperation and collaboration creates an additional incentive to create relationships, not only with other systems librarians, but with other departments and other institutions. When you embark on one of these collaborative efforts, ensure that your own institution will be able to reap some of the benefits—whether directly or in terms of publicity, good will, or increased use of electronic resources you wish to promote. Remember also that you are representing your entire library in many of these projects; and do not promise more than you can deliver. If you need to involve your library's administration in order to secure funding or institutional permission to proceed, do so, and make sure you are all on the same page.

Developing good networking skills will serve you well in every aspect of your career in systems librarianship. Foster your connections with others carefully, and always remember that you are part of a number of larger communities.

Works Cited

1. Thomas C. Wilson. *The Systems Librarian: Designing Roles, Defining Skills.* Chicago: ALA Editions, 1998: 163.

2. Heiberger, Mary Morris, and Julia Miller Vick. "Networking for Dummies." *The Chronicle of Higher Education*, May 17, 2002. 19 May 2002 (http://chronicle.com/jobs/2002/05/2002051701c.htm).

Chapter 6

Instruction Techniques

"Learning can be defined as the process of remembering what you are interested in. And both go hand in hand—warm hand in warm hand—with communication."
—Richard Saul Warman[1]

Bibliographic instruction has always been one of librarians' basic tasks; we understand that it is less than desirable—and less than fair—to maintain buildings full of valuable resources without also providing the opportunity for our patrons to develop the skills to locate and make use of those resources. Given that we are more often than not accessing newer resources strictly online (through, for example, Web-based OPACs and electronic databases), we now have a responsibility to our patrons to provide them with opportunities to learn to use today's library effectively. This means that we need to extend our traditional experience with bibliographic instruction to also include technology instruction, from teaching basic Windows skills and Internet usage to providing training on specific databases or more advanced search techniques. While some librarians may worry that teaching technological literacy is tangential to the library's mission, it is our responsibility to give people the tools they need to participate in our institutions. Our interest in inculcating technological literacy extends our traditional interest in literacy and in information-seeking skills.

Staff members may also require training in these general areas, as well as on use of the various modules of your automation system and on other library-specific technologies. In many libraries, you will find that technology has been added and upgraded bit by bit over the years but that staff have been provided with little formal training on its use, and have had either little time to learn the ins and outs of library technology or little interest in developing skills on their own. In any library, staff will be at a variety of stages of technological savvy. Librarians, however, cannot realistically be expected to provide adequate service to patrons in a wired institution if they have never been given the tools to use technology effectively themselves. One of your responsibilities as a systems librarian will be to bring up the skill levels of others in your organization. If sufficient training has not been provided in the past, you will also need to make up for your institution's previous shortcomings. As Karen Schneider notes: "Some of these people [library staff] never recovered from the shock of having computers plunked down in their work areas without any accompanying rationale or training."[2]

In many cases, you and/or other systems staff will be able to provide in-house training for your coworkers. In other cases, you may wish to locate and send staff to affordable and reputable outside courses or bring in outside trainers for specific software packages. You can also use a combination of these methods, as appropriate for your needs. On large systems such as your ILS, vendors may supply training for at least a limited number of people, and it never hurts to ask about the potential for vendor training or demos for staff when you invest in a new subscription database or other expensive electronic library product.

As a systems librarian, therefore, you will likely be involved either directly as a trainer during patron and staff computer instructional sessions, or with formulating the syllabus, methods, and format of such instruction. You will furthermore often encounter opportunities to do more informal on-demand training, demonstrating on the spur of the moment how to accomplish a computer-related task, or creating handouts and cheat sheets aimed at empowering library staff and users to carry out such tasks independently. The effectiveness of all of these instructional activities goes back to your library background and your communication skills; as University of Washington systems librarian Emalee Craft notes: "As a librarian, a lot of my skills involve how to communicate effectively with users in a way that will help fill their information needs. I think these same skills have been invaluable in relating technological terms and ideas to other staff members and users of the library."

Adult Learners

Training adult learners requires a different approach than you may have been used to in high school and other classes. Adult learners, first and foremost, need to be convinced of the advantages that training will bring to them personally. If adult learners are not self-motivated and not convinced of the value of training, they will not learn. This is as true of your patrons as it is of your staff. Along with self-motivation, realize that adult learners also place a high value on their time, which they will not wish to feel is being wasted. When training adults, refrain from spending a great deal of time on buildup or on covering material that is impractical or irrelevant to your trainees' immediate needs; they will merely tune you out. Particularly when it comes to technology training, you need to keep sessions practical and to the point. Avoid both theory and jargon as much as possible, and try to relate training back to concrete examples of how they can use what you are showing them in their jobs or in their daily lives.

Adult learners also tend to learn best by analogy. They have had years to develop their knowledge and a mental map of their world, and the best way to reach them is by demonstrating the parallels between what you are trying to teach and what they already know. Show how an e-mail address is analogous to a postal address, for example, or let users who are already familiar with the game play Windows Solitaire to develop their skills with the mouse. Understand that turning over a "card" on the computer screen equates easily to turning over a physical card, and that the more of these connections you can help your trainees, especially beginners, make to their pre-existing stores of knowledge, the more comfortable they will be with using new technology.

Lastly, it is important to develop training skills alongside your skills with technology. Merely knowing the ins and outs of a particular program is insufficient. Realize that many adult learners will be uncomfortable with or fearful of technology; computers hold a peculiar mystique in the minds of many adult learners, which you will need to work to overcome. Always keep in mind what it is like to confront a program—or a PC—for the first time, and try to empathize with your trainees. Cultivate patience along with the communication skills discussed in Chapter 1.

Training Techniques

It is important to take into account the different learning styles of individuals in your training sessions. Attendees tend to be at their best when learning in different ways; some, for example, may be highly visual learners and will benefit from seeing PowerPoint slides and other visual aids, while others may be auditory learners and will need to hear you explain a skill or process. Use a mixture of different methods in combination with hands-on practice in any training program, and provide self-study materials for those who would prefer to learn on their own or to supplement training with individual study.

Always allow time for staff and patrons to review the material you have provided. For staff, this can mean working with department heads to set aside time for their staff to practice on their own following a training session. For patrons, this can mean reserving some time for hands-on practice at the end of a training session, or providing an environment where they can come in to review later. To this end, you can consider posting training materials on your Web site and providing handouts that trainees can take with them to review on their own time. Always be sure to supply review materials and printed cheat sheets that show, step-by-step, how to accomplish the common computer-related tasks that you have demonstrated in your training sessions. If possible, test these cheat sheets on someone without previous knowledge of how to complete the task, to ensure that you do not leave out any steps. (Handouts will also be useful in the case of technical or equipment failure; at least attendees will not leave empty-handed, and you can use handouts to discuss at least some of the points you originally intended to cover.)

Keep handouts and training simple, as short as possible, and to the point. Remember that adult learners want to feel that they are using their time wisely, and will not appreciate having to wade through superfluous and distracting information to find out what they need to know. Computers can be confusing enough without your adding to the situation! Try to create an environment where trainees feel comfortable asking questions. You do not want attendees coming away confused or feeling as if they did not learn what they came for. Often trainees will come to a class with a specific goal or question in mind, which, although it may not be specifically what you intended to teach, will be useful to them in their daily lives or work. If such a question is appropriate and relevant to the subject at hand, answer it. If it is too tangential, offer to talk with the person after the training session. This allows you to avoid holding up the class with too much extraneous information, while still showing your receptivity to trainees' needs. Pay attention to students, making eye contact and noting those who are looking "lost" during the class. If they are reluctant to ask questions, ask specifically if they would like a point clarified. Some will feel embarrassed exposing what they see as their own ignorance in front of other trainees; be sensitive to this possibility and never make a questioner feel a query is either inappropriate or uninformed.

Create realistic objectives for your training sessions, teach directly to these objectives, and make sure that they are achievable in the time allotted. Computer training objectives need to be specific, practical, and measurable; you can see, for example, whether an attendee at a basic public Internet training class can now type a Web address into Internet Explorer to go to a site on the Internet. You can observe whether, post-training, a member of the reference staff can now place a hold in the appropriate module of your new ILS. Keep the number of objectives for any one class low; you cannot inculcate technological literacy in a single session. It will be more useful to present the same few objectives from several angles than to cram multiple objectives into a limited amount of time; repetition increases retention.

Training Staff

Training library staff members on computer usage presents a peculiar set of challenges. In any given library, the staff's level of technical competency and comfort with change will vary greatly. Some staff members may have graduated recently and picked up a strong set of technical skills in a revamped library or information school program. Some may have graduated years ago before such skills were taught regularly, or were taught then-current technologies such as punch cards and Apple BASIC that are less than relevant in the modern environment. These librarians have had to learn technical skills on the job (or have avoided learning them on the job). Paraprofessional staff either may have an extensive technical background but lack the foundation in librarianship to go with it, or may have worked in a library for years without receiving any formal training in or increasing their own comfort with technology. While library administrations increasingly desire technical skills in new employees, the wider range of options and salaries available to technically adept MLS holders means that those with these skills often go elsewhere—and the changing nature of library technology means that even those who enter with such abilities will at some point need their skills upgraded or refreshed.

In a larger institution, you can find yourself needing to establish classes at various levels and to accommodate various learning styles. (This is integral; pairing more advanced learners with beginners only serves to frustrate both groups, as you waste the time of those who already know the material and convince novices of their own ignorance compared to others.) This is a situation in which your competency checklists will come in handy, giving you a tool to assess the skill levels of various staff members and match them up with their peers.

Furthermore, with some staff members, you may face the challenge of convincing them of the need for training in the first place. If staff go into training sessions with the mindset that they have already mastered all of the skills they need to adequately serve patrons, whether in library school or through their years on the job, they will be less likely to retain material from technology training, and will be less likely to revisit the skills they have learned after sessions have ended (which is an essential factor in retaining knowledge). If they go in viewing computers as toys, interlopers, or machines that constantly break or otherwise frustrate their "real" work, they will not be receptive to learning. Your first task with such staff members, therefore, will be to convince them that training is indeed important and that a certain level of comfort and facility with technology is now essential to serving patrons effectively.

When training those who are less than convinced of the value of computer technology in serving patrons or serving the needs of the library, it is important to show them how their new skills can be put into practice in their daily tasks. This can best be accomplished through concrete examples; show how specific patron questions can be resolved, for example, through the use of a new online database. Ask for suggestions of real-life problems or questions staff have encountered, and show how computer technology can help resolve those problems. Provide scheduled times to practice these new skills after the session, so that staff do not feel that they are taking time away from their job to spend on technology. Provide follow-up sessions for staff to reinforce the skills they have learned and give them an opportunity to share any instances in which their new knowledge has helped them on the job. Create online tutorials or practice sessions and post them on your intranet to help staff develop their skills outside of formal training sessions. Create printed handouts to distribute at your sessions, as well as printed cheat sheets, assessments, and exercises that they can use at their own pace—remember, those who are less familiar with technology might also be more comfortable with using print resources.

Additionally, training should be just one component in an entire campaign to convince staff of the importance of technology in the day-to-day running of the modern library and to familiarize them with technology as an everyday concept. Remember from previous chapters the importance of communication in imparting the value of technology and in minimizing your co-workers' fear of change. Use venues such as a technology tips newsletter, your library intranet, and informal conversation to help show others how technology can be used effectively and how it is intertwined with daily library operations. If you have created technology competencies for staff, show how knowledge of these particular areas can help make their jobs easier. One common complaint about technology training is that it takes time away from an already short workday, especially in those institutions facing declining staffing levels and increasing workloads.

(Ironically, the expense of keeping up technologically can exacerbate these staffing issues.) Showing how familiarity with various aspects of the library's technological environment can in the long run make staff's jobs easier and allow them to complete tasks and/or help patrons more quickly will go a long way toward countering such objections.

As your training program progresses, staff who have benefited from earlier training sessions will be more receptive to future opportunities. Much of the stress inherent in dealing with technology in libraries comes from a feeling of not being able to keep up, of the lack of knowledge of how to use and deal with these resources. By giving staff the tools to not only deal with computers but also to integrate technology into their daily lives, you can tremendously reduce that level of anxiety and help them deal with the inevitable changes to come. You also help reduce the digital divide among staff members—which we worry greatly about among our patrons, but sometimes neglect to pay attention to among our own staff. Merely providing access to technology is insufficient if staff are not prepared to use and benefit from such technology; the gap between those who are informed about, welcome, and use computers and those who do not can seem as insurmountable as the gap between those who have access to the Internet or to computing technology and those who do not.

While some staff may resist learning about technology, others will welcome the opportunity—and well thought-out training opportunities can also be a selling point for your library when it comes to hiring and retaining staff. Libraries that invest in their staff's professional development, including technical development, will in the long run serve both staff and patrons more effectively. As Bruce Massis points out: "Any library that makes the decision to provide and promote continuing technology education will reap the rewards of better hires, increased retention of qualified staff, and improved customer service."[3] Make sure also to provide training opportunities to new hires who may begin their positions some time after formal training is completed on a new product or service; it is unfair to expect them to pick up the usage of a system on an ad hoc basis when everyone else has received training. If you are in a larger institution, you may consider creating a training program specifically for new employees, or you can tailor their training on a more personalized basis after they have completed your set of competency tests.

While your role in creating and facilitating training is integral, note that in-house training may be only one component. A forward-thinking library should also make it possible for staff to pursue outside continuing education opportunities—and should especially encourage systems librarians and other technical staff to take advantage of appropriate opportunities to shore up their skills. (For more on finding classes for you and other systems staff, see Chapter 7.)

Try to make it as easy as possible for staff to participate in technology training sessions. To avoid overload and for the sake of others' scheduling convenience, consider varying your class offerings. As a supplement to longer classes, you might, for instance, provide short, half-hour sessions once a week on specific topics such as e-mail basics or new ILS features. Staff can attend as needed to shore up their skills. Provide online tutorials on your intranet to supplement in-person training, so that your coworkers can learn or practice on their own. (See more on creating online training later in this chapter.) This will be especially useful to part-timers who may not easily be able to adjust their schedules to attend in-person training sessions. Coordinate with department heads and supervisors so that they understand the value and necessity of both training itself and allowing staff time to review on their own later, and try to work your class offerings into their schedules. You want to remove as many obstacles to training as you can.

Training Patrons

Patron training presents its own set of opportunities and challenges to the systems librarian/trainer. Patrons who attend computer classes at the library may be more self-motivated than staff, who often attend classes only because it is required, rather than out of any inherent interest in the subject. This in some ways makes patrons easier to teach. Again, however, you will see a disparity in knowledge levels and expectations among patrons attending any computer classes you offer. Those who have not grown up with computers or who have never learned basic skills may seek introductory Windows, word processing, and Internet training—or even just instruction on using a mouse—while those who are computer savvy might benefit more from instruction on the use of your library's electronic databases and other online resources.

Many libraries, therefore, might need to provide a variety of training sessions to patrons at different levels of computer expertise. The type and number of classes you offer will vary from library to library; some may choose simply to offer training sessions on the Internet and/or the use of the library's OPAC and other electronic resources, while others may create full-fledged training programs on topics such as creating documents with Office software and using Microsoft Windows. It is up to you and/or your institution to determine how the goal of teaching technological literacy fits into the library's broader mission, and what can realistically be supported with the staff and resources you have available.

Ad Hoc Opportunities

Be alert to opportunities to do one-on-one, ad hoc training when the occasion presents itself. Many computer situations present a learning opportunity, and even the process of resolving a problem with someone's computer allows you an opening to explain why and how you are performing certain actions. Often, these informal occasions for learning can be more productive than a formal session, and those you are helping may learn without being aware that they are being taught. Computer users also may feel more comfortable asking questions one-to-one than during a more formal training session.

Ad hoc opportunities also provide the perfect environment for hands-on training, from which users are more likely to benefit. When you are showing someone how to accomplish a task or resolve a minor issue, avoid taking over their machine if at all possible. Let them sit at the terminal, type, and click for themselves. Even if you are showing them how to proceed at every step, they will gain a feeling of accomplishment that they have "done it themselves" and will be more likely to remember the steps if they need to repeat the process later. If you explain the "why" behind your actions as you are showing them how to proceed, this will help them retain the steps as well. Patience is an essential attribute for a successful computer trainer; you have to be willing to watch users struggle, resist the urge to simply do tasks for them, and develop a sense of when and how it is appropriate to intervene.

Setting Up Sessions

The actual format of your training sessions may depend largely on the equipment and facilities you have available. If you have the opportunity to be involved in the design of an actual training or computer lab, seize that chance with delight. Consider factors from room temperature and ambient noise, to whether students can see a trainer from behind their monitors, to standardizing on consistent hardware and software, to whether you wish to purchase classroom control software that allows a trainer to push materials to student desktops and keep them from indulging in off-topic activities such as games and checking e-mail while you are trying to conduct a session. Products here include LanSchool (http://www.lanschool.com) and Net-Support School (http://www.netsupport- inc.com), although there are a number of alternatives to choose from.

If your library lacks a computer lab, you will need to be more creative in adapting to available resources. Do not use the lack of formal training facilities, however, as an excuse not to provide any instruction. If you need to cluster smaller groups around one or two terminals, do so. Training sessions taught in this manner will of necessity seem more informal and will reach fewer people at a time, but they may also have the advantage of being less threatening for beginners and those who are fearful of the technology.

The space you have available will necessarily influence the format and size of your classes. If you have a projector and lab available, you might wish to use PowerPoint to demonstrate your points and then provide an opportunity for hands-on practice. If you are clustering people around one terminal, you will probably wish to avoid PowerPoint and lecturing and simply demonstrate techniques. As always, be flexible and willing to adapt to the technology at hand.

Online Training

One of the advantages of working in a "wired institution" is that it provides an environment for you to post training and other tools online. This allows staff and patrons to pursue learning on their own time. Examples of training materials you can provide on the Web or on your intranet include tutorials, quizzes, help documents, and competency self-assessments. You can also easily link to other online resources to give people the chance to read further on a technical topic of interest. While often not a complete substitute for in-person training, online training can help supplement your in-person efforts, provide an opportunity for people to practice their skills, and reach people who may be unwilling to attend a more formal session. These materials also allow staff or patrons to engage in self-paced learning and to practice at their own convenience.

There are a number of useful tools that can assist you in creating online training materials. You can keep these online resources as simple as step-by-step instructions, with screenshots, on accomplishing common tasks, or you can create interactive quizzes and video tutorials for intranet or Web site users. (A useful tool for screen captures is TechSmith's SnagIt, at http://www.techsmith.com.) There are a number of cost-effective options that will help you post-training materials online, some of which are add-ins or extensions to software you might already own. See for example:

- *Macromedia's CourseBuilder extension for Dreamweaver*: http://www.macromedia.com/software/coursebuilder. This free extension allows you to create multiple choice, true/false, and drag-and-drop quizzes and publish results to databases.

- *Microsoft PowerPoint 2002 Producer Add-In*: http://office. microsoft.com/downloads/2002/producer.aspx. Allows you to create rich-media slides and publish them to the Web. Note that PowerPoint's ability to output HTML versions of its slides in itself provides the opportunity to publish tutorials online.

- *TechSmith's Camtasia*: http://www.techsmith.com/ products/camtasia/camtasia.asp. Create recordings of your computer interactions; includes the ability to add an audio track so that you can simultaneously explain your actions.

- *Testcraft Standard Edition*: http://www.testcraft.com/ FeaSTD.asp. Allows easy creation of online assessments and includes a number of reporting options.

Systems librarians with a high comfort level with Web scripting or programming might also choose to create their own tests and tools without relying on third-party options. If you wish to keep things simple, you can create straight HTML tutorials sans interactivity—although these might be most useful as "cheat sheets," or step-by-step instructions on straightforward tasks. If you use PowerPoint presentations during your training sessions, you can easily convert these to HTML and post them online.

When considering how best to create and format your online offerings, it will be helpful to examine what other institutions have done. Examples include the University of Texas's TILT ("Texas Information Literacy Tutorial") at http://tilt.lib.utsystem.edu (see Figure 6.1) and the Washoe County Library System's tutorial on mouse use at http://www.washoe.lib.nv.us/pub_mouse.html.

If you wish to post a tutorial or quizzes on a particular software package, ask your colleagues in other institutions or inquire on appropriate mailing lists whether others have created online

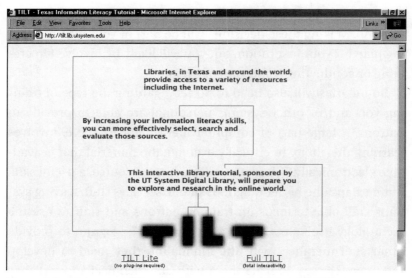

Figure 6.1   University of Texas Information Literacy Tutorial (TILT)

training materials on a similar topic, and see how theirs are structured before creating your own.

Setting Boundaries

Systems librarians must learn to make tough decisions as to how much and what type of training they can realistically provide to both staff and patrons. This is especially important for those working in a smaller library and for solo systems librarians. You may choose, for example, to give public service staff members the skills to teach Internet, OPAC, and basic word processing classes to patrons themselves, rather than trying to personally conduct all such training. You may provide staff members with training on library-specific applications such as ILS modules but require them to do some self-study or to take outside classes on applications such as Microsoft Word, Excel, or your business office's accounting package. This approach also lessens your burden of learning all these applications sufficiently to teach them to others, when in-depth knowledge of these specific packages is not integral to your own job. Making these decisions will be part of your overall training plan for your institution, but you will likely be involved in creating or conducting some kind of training.

Boundaries will also need to be set regarding the type of training you and/or other systems personnel are able to provide to patrons. A large part of computer literacy, for example, involves learning the ability to critically evaluate the material that is available electronically. Information literacy is, of course, a useful skill, but perhaps one better taught by public services staff, leaving systems staff able to focus on training patrons and staff to use the technology itself. Set up a "train the trainer" program to provide other staff members with the foundation they need to develop their own classes. Provide them with any technical support they require, posting their training materials online or demonstrating the use of classroom control software, for example, but let them control the format and content of their training sessions. Remember that you and your colleagues are on the same side, and part of providing them the tools to deploy technology effectively involves providing the skills to pass those tools on to others.

Again, your communication, people, and library skills will come in handy here. IT people can have a hard time "letting go" and allowing others to take control of technology, but librarians understand that knowledge shared only grows.

Works Cited

1. Warman, Richard Saul. *Information Anxiety 2*. Indianapolis: Que, 2001: 249.

2. Schneider, Karen. "The Old Guard and the New Technology." *Library Journal*, March 1, 1994: 64.

3. Massis, Bruce E. "How to Create and Implement a Technology Training Program." *American Libraries*, October 2001: 49.

Chapter 7

Independent Study

> *"… what we should take with us from library
> school is the ability to keep learning, to be com-
> fortable trying new and difficult and sometimes
> threatening things, and to know that whatever we
> don't know, we can learn."*
>
> —Mary Ellen Bates[1]

Since library school cannot teach everything associated with
systems librarianship, and since technology changes rapidly
enough to make merely keeping up a constant challenge, one of
your most important responsibilities as a systems librarian will be
to keep yourself current with the latest tools and techniques necessary to do your job effectively. The one certainty of systems
librarianship is that there is always something more to learn,
although the specific technologies you need to master will, as
always, vary depending on your institution and environment.
Luckily, there are a number of options for extending your education beyond library school and giving yourself the tools you need
to remain up-to-date.

Your foundation in the practices and principles of librarianship, built from library school coursework and from your professional activities, will inform the way you integrate the
technological knowledge you acquire into your day-to-day tasks.
Because of this, it is less important that you learn the use of specific technologies in library school or before becoming a systems
librarian than that you embrace the capacity to learn and the
principles of our profession. As Herbert White explains: "[Library
school] educators must recognize that if programs stress only the

how of technological applications, then no matter how current the course, the student's learning will be obsolete in two years. It is far more important that we stress the *why* of technology in the context of our own responsibilities."[2] Try to learn something new every day, and always be open to the possibility of expanding your personal knowledge base. Your attitude and flexibility will allow you to gain the skills and information you need to adapt to new technological opportunities.

One truism of library work is that there is never enough money for everything your institution would like to purchase. Unfortunately, this lack of funding also often extends to funding for education, so many systems librarians find themselves needing to argue for institutional support for formal computer training. As one somewhat frustrated survey respondent notes: "Public libraries often do not have the finances or the commitment to keeping their systems people well-trained and up-to-date. Many library managers attended school 20 or more years ago and have not kept up with the developments in technology. They often are not committed to finding the financing for their systems or the training for their systems people to keep their libraries on the cutting edge." Technology classes can also often be costly, which exacerbates the unwillingness of library administrations to spend a seemingly disproportionate amount of their training budget on technical coursework.

The following sections describe several ways of overcoming this funding gap (which is not unique to public libraries) and keeping current with new technological developments and changes in your institution's computing environment. These include locating free and low-cost online classes and tutorials, attending inexpensive local workshops or computer training center and community college courses, self-education, and current awareness. Note that several of these options also lend themselves as training alternatives for your staff; you can encourage the use of online tutorials and

attendance at local training sessions, for example, as your coworkers begin to master your institution's set of computer competencies. Because free and low-cost options might not always be
sufficient, however, also find a discussion of finding and arguing
for the funding for training opportunities, including writing such
funding into technology grant applications.

Other options for systems learning include attending local and
national conferences and user group meetings, as well as joining
and reading appropriate e-mail discussion lists. (See more on
groups, meetings, and online participation in Chapter 5.)
Remember that every conference session and presentation you
attend and each post you peruse is a potential learning opportunity; our best teachers are generally our colleagues who have faced
similar challenges. Make a conscious effort to keep continuously
learning and "keeping up" a priority—it is easy to allow the activities in this chapter to fall by the wayside when involved in seemingly more pressing day-to-day dilemmas. But a commitment to
lifelong learning will allow you to remain both effective in your day-
to-day work and current in a changing technological environment.

Online Classes and Tutorials

Reflecting the way in which computer technology has woven
itself into every aspect of our lives, there are now an abundance of
free and low-cost online classes and tutorials that serve the needs
of those wishing to learn more about using such technology. While
a number of these online offerings are addressed to end-users with
limited previous technical knowledge, there are also a variety of
affordable options for systems librarians who wish to improve
their knowledge of a certain product or to acquire new skills such
as programming or advanced Web design techniques.

Free/Low-Cost Online Classes/Tutorials

The following Web sites each contain a number of technology courses and/or tutorials on a variety of topics. For opportunities focused on a particular vendor's technology, also check the vendor's own Web site and watch its e-mail discussion list and press releases, or do an online search for tutorials on a specific topic.

- *Barnes & Noble University*: http://www.barnesandnoble university.com. Find computer courses in their science and technology section. Classes (from "Beginning Web Animation with Macromedia Flash" to "Programming Basics") are free: You are encouraged to buy textbooks through B&N, but librarians know the power of interlibrary loan. Communicate with the instructor and fellow students via online forums.

- *FindTutorials.com*: http://www.findtutorials.com. A $99 yearly membership purchases access to 357 downloadable IT training courses; also find hundreds of free online tutorials.

- *Learn2*: http://www.tutorials.com. Prices vary depending on the tutorial; includes both online and CD-ROM options. Tutorials are fairly basic, and free samples are available online.

- *Learnthat.com*: http://www.learnthat.com/courses/ computer. Hundreds of free animated tutorials on topics from Linux to Microsoft Access, and practice questions for certification exams such as A+.

- *OCLC Institute*: http://institute.oclc.org. Technical areas (general, MCSE, and Web development) each cost $110 per year for access to all self-paced courses in the series. Sample courses available.

- *TechTutorials*: http://www.techtutorials.com. Free, searchable computer tutorials and white papers collected from around the Web.

- *Trainingtools.com*: http://trainingtools.com. Class previews are free; $135/year purchases communication with the instructor, discussions, downloadable courses, and additional functionality.

- *W3Schools Online*: http://www.w3schools.com. Free tutorials and quizzes on Web development topics.

These sites are just a sampling of the online technical coursework and tutorials available; look also for sites devoted to learning specific topics or software packages.

Beyond checking general online sources for learning about technology, systems librarians should also look for Internet-based classes at their local library systems, associations, and user groups. A number of these groups are posting tutorials online, Webcasting seminars, and expanding into Web-based instruction. These groups' offerings sometimes have the advantage of teaching technological skills from a library perspective, and in this sense they might be preferred over more general options. They are also often subsidized by the sponsoring system or group, and thus they are more affordable than the online classes offered by library schools and computer training centers. (For more on taking advantage of local opportunities, see the Local Workshops section later in this chapter.)

National library associations and organizations are also beginning to offer technology-related tutorials and coursework online. New in 2002, for example, is the OCLC Institute's Online Library Learning series of cost-effective computer courses (see sidebar). The Institute offers these courses in partnership with MindLeaders in a variety of technical areas, including end-user classes on applications, general technical tutorials, MCSE courses, and technical Web development. The free demo courses provided on their site can help you assess whether their courses (or online learning in general) might be useful to you; also consider whether online classwork might be a helpful supplement to the in-person training you are able to provide for other library staff members, and be sure to examine end-user as well as more technical offerings. ARL's Online Lyceum (http://www.arl.org/arl/workshops.html) provides another source for online coursework in topics such as designing accessible Web pages and licensing electronic information products.

An Interview with OCLC Institute Executive Director Erik Jul (May 2002)

Could you tell me a little bit about the OCLC Institute and its mission?

Seven years ago, the OCLC board of trustees decided it was appropriate for OCLC to extend its mission of serving libraries and librarians through education. In 1996, it established the OCLC Institute, and our first offering was in June that same year. Like OCLC itself, the OCLC Institute's mission is to promote the evolution of libraries, but specifically through advanced education and knowledge exchange. We take a global view, providing opportunities for working professionals worldwide and focusing on continuing education for the adult learner.

We offer three types of educational opportunities:

1) Instructor-led seminars, which typically reach 25–30 attendees over one to two and a half days. These are intended to be graduate-level seminars, and may combine hands-on work with lectures and demonstrations as well as small-group discussions and presentations.

2) Larger forums such as conferences and pre-conference workshops, which we offer once to twice a year. Examples include the OCLC/ARL Strategic Issues Forum and the upcoming Virtual Reference Desk Conference.

3) Distance learning opportunities, for which we have previously developed content directly related to the standards, art, and practice of librarianship. (An example of this is our course, "Cataloging Internet Resources Using MARC 21 and AACR2.") This course has enjoyed rapid acceptance, albeit among a specialized group of cataloging professionals. Recently, we expanded our offerings by partnering with MindLeaders, a leader in distance education with a particularly strong catalog of technology courses. We are currently focusing on technical classes because technical skills are now a key part of all jobs in libraries, from using office applications, to library administration, to library systems. Technology knowledge allows librarians to accomplish their mission of service to their communities.

Is all of this new technical course content created entirely by MindLeaders?

Yes—this is a strategic partnership with a third-party provider, and content is directly related to end-user desktop computing and programming/systems administration.

What type of response have you received from librarians to your announcement of these courses' availability?

We went live with these courses on April 24, 2002, and made a general announcement on around 12 library-oriented lists as well as on our own Web page. This was the only publicity we have done so far, and it resulted in our largest-ever single day spike in Web traffic—we started seeing hits literally minutes after our message went out, and traffic accelerated from there. This seems a pretty good indication of initial interest.

Obviously, visitors will want to explore, get more information, and see how the courses meet their needs and their job requirements, but we did see first-day sales in each group of classes that we offer.

Is this initiative envisioned as a solution for individual librarians, or for libraries wishing to offer low-cost technical training to employees?

Really for both. Our current online sales method supports individual learners, but we also accommodate group sales—from the staff development director who wants to purchase on behalf of staff in a single library to an entire local, state, or regional library system or consortium. We see a role both for the individual learner and for those who are given the opportunity to learn by their employer, and we support both.

Are all current MindLeaders courses self-paced tutorials?

Yes, all are currently self-paced and asynchronous, allowing learners to learn wherever and whenever it is convenient. The courses themselves are mounted on computers at OCLC, which means users benefit from a secure, redundant, and highly reliable computing environment. With greater than

99.9 percent system reliability, users really can expect to be able to learn at any time around the clock.

Do these courses have specific technical requirements?

There are few requirements beyond Internet access and a current Web browser. Some courses will require the use of common plugins such as QuickTime and Real Audio, but all are also available as text-only courses (which also makes them broadly accessible).

Why should librarians take these courses through OCLC rather than through one of the other vendors providing online technical tutorials?

OCLC Institute's major role here is to bring awareness of these opportunities. We have a reach, stability, and name awareness that others don't, and want to extend these offerings through our OCLC Network partners, regional service centers, and international divisions. Libraries are familiar with OCLC and their local OCLC service provider, and we wanted it to be easy and convenient for users to discover and subscribe to MindLeaders courses.

We also want to bring these courses to a market we care about and are personally involved with, whereas other online course vendors may have little or no long-term experience in library operations and library applications. Will they be in business tomorrow, will they support online learning like we will, and do they offer the same reliability?

Lastly, we appreciate the opportunity to offer these courses at a very attractive price. If librarians were to purchase single courses directly from MindLeaders or another vendor, the cost might rapidly become prohibitive. But our subscription pricing allows individuals the advantages of a group buying-power without having to be part of a giant organization. We didn't want price to be a barrier to anyone.

(Note: a list of MindLeaders technical courses and additional information can be found at http://institute.oclc.org.)

Online coursework can, of course, be supplemented with in-person classes, independent study of print resources, and on-the-job experience. Any systems librarian, however, should develop a certain level of comfort with online learning, both through formal online training sessions and through independent reading and self-paced tutorials. We of all people cannot afford to neglect the opportunities technology itself affords us for learning.

Community College and Computer Training Center Classes

Community colleges and local computer training centers offer the opportunity to take in-person technical training classes, in situations where you would prefer a more hands-on or instructor-led approach than may be available online. While courses that are part of a certification track (such as Microsoft's MSCE or the A+ certification for computer technicians) may be somewhat pricier than others, overall costs are generally reasonable. Comparison shop and examine course outlines to see if the classes are likely to meet your needs. These outlines can sometimes be found online; also watch for community colleges' printed class schedules in the mail or request syllabi/outlines from the school itself.

Note that computer training centers do gear many of their course offerings toward those seeking technical certification.

While there is nothing inherently wrong with such classes, realize that they may tend to "teach to the test," rather than focusing on the tasks that will be specifically useful in your daily activities, and that they will of course lack a library focus. If you do intend to take a number of courses in one area of study, however, you might wish to investigate the possibility of becoming certified in a subject that is relevant to your institution's needs. Your employer might also be more likely to fund classes toward certification than it will be to fund general computer training courses, since these classes are more easily compared to the MLS and LTA classwork that the institution may already be accustomed to paying for.

Certifications are also one way to prove to your employer that you take your systems responsibilities seriously, and any continuing education will provide you with a concrete base from which to argue for increased compensation. (For more on compensation, see Chapter 9.) As survey respondent Eric Elmore, automated services librarian at Texas A&M suggests: "Start working to earn outside certifications as soon as possible. A+, Novell, or Microsoft Network Certifications, etc. They ... show levels of competence that make employers confident and the sooner you start the better off you will be, and the more money you can command for your skills."

Computer training centers are also now moving into the online market, offering their traditional in-person courses remotely in order to expand their customer base. Examine these courses carefully to ensure that you will receive the same instructor attention and interaction as you would if attending a class at the center's physical facility. Be wary of paying the same prices for online classes that are basically the equivalent of self-paced tutorials, as such tutorials are generally widely available elsewhere at little or no cost. While in-person courses may seem to require you to invest more time by sitting in a class, the hands-on experience and instructor attention can be worth it, especially when it comes to technical courses.

The most basic way to locate local computer training centers is by looking under "Computer Training" in a good online phone directory. See if the center has a Web site, and look at the quality of its design and organization as a possible indication of the quality of the coursework. (A technical school should have a useful and useable site!) Check for articles on the company, see if others have reported on their experiences, consult other systems librarians in your area to see if they have used a particular training center, and use any other means possible to investigate a training center's reputation and reliability. Especially if you intend to take a number of courses at one training center, be sure to investigate before enrolling. See, if possible, if a training center is in good financial shape, as some failing institutions have been known to shut their doors without refunding students' tuition. Ask if you can audit or sit in on part of a class to assess the quality of training before enrolling in a course. Some centers will give prospective customers certificates for free sample classes, although you will have to choose from their lower-cost (most likely end-user) offerings.

Also examine continuing education opportunities at your local community college, which are generally listed separately from the college's courses for matriculated students. Continuing education courses are usually geared more toward working adults than are classes for those enrolled full-time; they are ideally focused on how technology is used in the "real world." Community college classes are also usually affordable and are often scheduled on nights and weekends to accommodate the largest number of continuing education students.

Local Workshops

Look for training opportunities provided throughout your state from your state library, large library systems/consortia, and your state library association. Keep in mind, however, that many computer training classes and workshops offered by consortia will be fairly basic, aimed at inculcating technical literacy in general library staff rather than at providing material that will be specifically useful to systems librarians. Examine the level of training advertised to see if you can view a class outline before registering for such workshops in order to avoid wasting your time covering topics you already know or that you could easily pick up from a book or by spending some time experimenting with the features of a piece of software.

The North Suburban Library System (NSLS), Illinois, for example, offers a number of continuing education workshops on computer-related issues (see catalog at http://www.nslsilus.org/ce). Classes range from those useful to systems librarians, such as "Project Management for IT Professionals," to those useful for other library staff, such as "Basic Microsoft Word 2000." What is particularly helpful about local systems' workshops is that, although they do maintain a focus on technical topics, they are geared specifically toward the use of that technology in a library setting. Other attendees are all working library staff. Further, coursework from NSLS and similar systems/consortia is extremely affordable; costs range from free to generally less than $100 per workshop. Local workshops also provide an opportunity to network with other professionals who are at least in one aspect at the same level of technological literacy as you.

Local technology user groups sometimes also feature low-cost workshops and speakers on technical topics—another reason to stay involved and keep informed. These groups will often advertise such opportunities in system or state library newsletters, and you may not need to be a member to attend. Note, however, that guest speakers will likely address broader trends rather than providing hands-on training. You may yourself consider offering to present at one of these groups, if you have a topic you would like to share with your fellow professionals.

Library Schools

While library school coursework is often one of the more expensive continuing education options, it can also be the most targeted to working systems librarians and will likely be taught from the library perspective. Distance continuing education courses might be the most useful for far-flung students. The offerings at the University of Wisconsin, Madison's School of Library and Information Studies (http://www.slis.wisc.edu/academic/ces), for example, often include courses in useful systems-related topics such as metadata, virtual collection development, and digitization. The University of Michigan's School of Information offers similar but on-site summer "Digital Tool Kits" (http://www.si.umich.edu/dtk) on topics from ColdFusion to technology trends for library managers. These courses also qualify for continuing education credit.

Check with your local library school as well, to see what it might offer in the way of continuing education coursework or certification classes. If you graduated from the institution, find out whether it offers alumni discounts on future courses. See whether you are able to take courses normally offered in the MLS track, if they are now offering newer technical classes or if you were unable to fit these in when pursuing the degree.

Self-Education

Any librarian should appreciate the power of reading and self-study. A number of resources are specifically geared toward self-education in the computer field, including test preparation guides for certifications such as the MCSE and Network+ and series such as the Sams "Teach Yourself ..." titles. If you purchase a new software package or upgrade to a new OS, take the time to work through the applicable self-study material in one of these resources. The hands-on exercises, quizzes, and review questions in these guides can help you gain valuable practice in a controlled setting before having to deal with an emergency situation under pressure.

Self-education also includes on-the-job learning. As you progress in your career as a systems librarian, each experience you have, whether setting up a new server, troubleshooting an annoying systems issue, or negotiating a contract with a database vendor, presents an opportunity for learning. Once you have done something once, you are more prepared to handle similar situations in the future. Each time you educate yourself when researching a systems issue or purchase, you extend your own technical knowledge base. If you are part of a larger systems department, you have the opportunity to learn from your colleagues and share knowledge and tips among one another. This on-the-job learning is often superior to any classroom training, and formal classwork, further, still requires you to practice your skills in the real world before you can truly claim competence.

If you are interested in expanding your skills in a certain area, set aside a regular block of time for practice and research. Give yourself the tools you need to learn. If you wish to extend your knowledge of open source software, for example, why not take an older machine you would otherwise discard, download Linux, and experiment with setting up and configuring the OS? Find other ways to practice and extend your skills before you need to use them in a real-world environment.

Current Awareness

The best way to continue your education as a systems librarian is to adopt a constant attitude of attentive awareness. If you have joined e-mail lists, if you read articles, if you hear an announcement on the radio, if you browse Web sites, always be on the lookout for information that might benefit the technological environment in your library. File useful e-mails into folders for future reference. Bookmark useful Web sites, file them, and rename them with descriptive names. Clip magazine articles and file them by subject. Then, when a situation arises in which your stored information becomes useful, you may not remember the solution offhand—but you will likely remember having seen it and be able to locate it easily in your personal knowledge management environment.

Online Opportunities

Due to their currency, frequently updated Internet resources are the best way to keep up-to-date on technological topics. You will wish, for example, to bookmark your favorite systems news Web sites and visit them regularly to find information on fast-moving topics such as virus alerts, new technologies, and security patches. If you take 15 minutes or so to browse news sites each morning, you will be less likely to miss important announcements that may affect your library and its users. Useful and frequently updated sites and Weblogs include:

- *ALA TechSource: The Source Online*: https://www.
  techsource.ala.org/index.pl. News and tips on technical
  issues for librarians. While much content is aimed at
  pushing their subscription products, you will also find
  useful news and links.

- *Library Techlog*: http://www.meberle.com/weblog.html.
  Matthew Eberle's Weblog specifically focuses on library

technology, often linking to stories, sites, and topics of interest to systems librarians.

- *LISNews.com*: http://www.lisnews.com. Blake Carver's broader Weblog focuses on issues for librarians and often discusses and links to information on technology topics.

- *SAPL Extra net*: http://extra.sapl.ab.ca. From the St. Albert Public Library, Extra net aims at "creating synergy between Librarians and Information Technology Specialists." Useful library tech news.

- *The Shifted Librarian*: http://www.theshiftedlibrarian. com. Jenny Levine's Weblog, containing news stories and commentary focusing on changes in the ways patrons and libraries receive information. A good source of new stories on e-books, PDAs, and applications of wireless technologies.

- *SysAds.org*: http://www.sysads.org. Stories are posted by site members, so you may wish to verify information through independent links, but you can also pick up information you may miss on more mainstream sites.

Supplement the sites in the list with your own favorites.

If you feel ambitious, you can also set up your own Weblog or other online resource to help keep you (and/or your peers) current on new technology trends. One of the more interesting innovations in Weblog technology is the ability to integrate Rich Site Summary (RSS) news feeds into your blog. Software packages such as Radio UserLand (http://radio.userland.com) include a news aggregator function that allows you to subscribe to free RSS feeds and choose the technology topics on which you wish to keep apprised. Relevant news blurbs and links will then appear on your personal news aggregator page, and you can pick which of these items to add to your blog. Even if you do not choose to make your Weblog public and instead just host it privately, or keep it on your personal

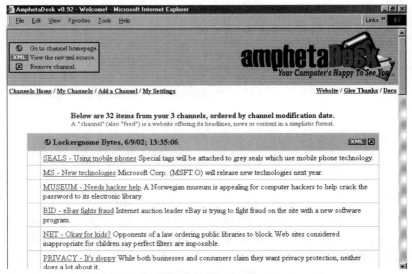

Figure 7.1   Sample RSS Feeds, Shown in AmphetaDesk

machine, you can use blogging software's RSS features to create your own searchable and commented technology knowledge and news base. You can also investigate open source news aggregators such as AmphetaDesk (http://www.disobey.com/amphetadesk), which create a personal news portal based on your own specifications (see Figure 7.1). Using RSS allows you to save time and collocate much of your daily reading in one place, and using AmphetaDesk or similar tools allows you to read directly through the aggregator as if you were visiting each of these Web sites.

Beyond Web sites, one of the best ways to keep current is by signing up to receive free e-mail newsletters on technology-related topics. These e-mailed newsletters help remove the burden of having to remember to go back to a site for the most current news, "pushing" articles, summaries, and tips directly to your e-mail box. On a daily or weekly basis, these newsletters can keep you aware of patches, virus alerts, tips, product releases, and ideas for using computer technology in your library. Be sure to sign up for general technical newsletters as well as library-related offerings. Some useful newsletters include:

- *Information Today NewsBreaks*: http://www.infotoday. com/newsbreaks/breaks.htm. Library-related breaking news, press releases, and conference reports.

- *InfoWorld*: http://www.iwsubscribe.com/newsletters. Windows, IT management issues, open source, Web technology, and networking are some relevant topics here.

- *LangaList*: http://www.langa.com/newsletter.htm. Tips on computer hardware, software, and online resources.

- *Lockergnome*: http://www.lockergnome.com. Choose from newsletters on Windows freeware, critical updates, Web sites, and news; IT reviews and troubleshooting advice; digital media; Linux projects; assistance; and cross-platform tools; Apple Mac tips and downloads; or Web design tips and reviews.

- *NetworkWorld*: http://www.nwwsubscribe.com/news. News alerts on network and systems administration topics, product reviews, wireless, IT education, technology Q&A, Linux, Novell, and Windows are only some of the offerings here.

- *Woody's Watch*: http://www.wopr.com. Weekly newsletters on Microsoft Office, Windows, Project, and Access.

Note that some of these sites allow you to sign up for a number of newsletters at once. Be selective, and if past issues are available online, read a couple to find out if the content looks useful to you before subscribing. Supplement the newsletters in the list with your own findings and/or those specific to technology used in your library.

Offline Opportunities

In your quest to become and remain self-educated, you will also likely wish to subscribe to topical computer-related print magazines (or to read or skim those to which your library subscribes), as well as to faithfully read publications such as *Computers in Libraries, Searcher, Library Hi-Tech,* and *Information Today,* which are specifically intended for information professionals in systems positions. Urge your institution to invest in subscriptions to the major library-related technology publications. Join library technology organizations such as LITA and read association journals such as *Information Technology and Libraries* and ASIST's *JASIST;* if you cannot afford to join, read the relevant selected articles that are made freely available online. The book reviews in such publications will give you further direction on avenues of self-study to help you improve your skills in supporting library technology.

As your name gets on mailing lists, you will also receive a number of solicitations to subscribe to free weeklies and monthlies such as *Network World* and *InfoWorld.* Take advantage of these offers! While much of the content of such publications might be irrelevant to your particular situation, you are bound to encounter useful articles. Furthermore, skimming these magazines on a regular basis allows you to keep abreast of new technological developments and will provide you with tips and tricks to better manage your computing environment. Do not feel you have to read each issue word-for-word, but do take even free publications seriously. Note that you can also sign up online to receive a number of free print publications; examples of these are *Government Technology* (http://www.govtech.net) and *Presentations Magazine* (http://www.presentations.com). If while surfing a relevant site you see such an offer, subscribe—you will likely have to fill out a long and annoying signup form, but the opportunities for learning make it worth your time. Do read free publications critically, however, as their dependence on advertising dollars can influence the slant of their articles. Again, use these resources in conjunction with others and with your existing store of knowledge. Realize that these types of magazines are usually a better source for keeping current with broad technical trends and for product and software reviews than for developing specific skills but that they have their place in your continuing quest to keep current.

An interesting way to see how others are keeping up is to look at sites like LITA's Tech Experts' Reading Habits at http://www.lita. org/committe/toptech/expertsread.htm, which lists the publications those on LITA's Top Tech Trends committee find useful. Ask your peers in other libraries what they read to keep current, and watch for suggestions on e-mail discussion lists. LITA's *Technology Electronic Reviews* (http://www.lita.org/ter), which reviews books and online resources on information technology topics, is another place to find pointers to useful material and information on items you might wish to add to your own reference bookshelf.

Funding Training Opportunities

While in an ideal world, all libraries would possess unlimited funding and all administrators would recognize the importance of lifelong learning, most librarians work under somewhat more realistic conditions, competing for a limited pool of funds. Unfortunately, a frequent byproduct of libraries' lack of sufficient funding is a tendency to skimp on professional development and training opportunities for library staff. While the methods described earlier in this chapter serve as lower-cost ways of bypassing this lack of funding, more formal and more costly classes and training opportunities also have their place.

If your institution already offers funding or full or partial tuition reimbursement for employees to attend library school, this will bolster your argument for receiving funding to attend computer training courses. These are equally as relevant to your job and your day-to-day duties as library school classes. Show how increasing your expertise will in the long run save your library the costs associated with system downtime, consulting fees, and repair.

If your library lacks a history of funding professional development opportunities, be prepared to point to pertinent studies and articles on increased employee retention and productivity among institutions that support continuing education. This will prove particularly effective if the library has grown dependent on your technological expertise and you can provide statistics on how a commitment to lifelong learning increases the retention of technical personnel.

Another way to fund technology training for yourself and for other staff members is to include training in any technology grant application you prepare. Most technology grants allow training as one of the areas they are willing to fund, so if you are intending to use grant money to expand technology-related programs or services, always make staff training part of the package. Also investigate nontechnology-specific grants that can be used for activities such as staff development or guest speakers—either of these can focus on technology training. Take full advantage of the training provided in any grant you receive, such as the training supplied with Gates Grants, which focuses on training library staff to use and teach the grant-provided equipment. Look at IMLS grants distributed through the states, at ALA-funded grants, and at funding provided by large technology companies and charitable institutions. Your library may want to subscribe to a resource like *Technology Grant News* (http://www.technology grantnews.com) or other grant publications to keep current on what funding is being offered.

Take advantage of any opportunity to extend your own learning and to encourage your institution to fund your technological professional development. Lifelong learning is essential to your success as a systems librarian.

Works Cited

1. Bates, Mary Ellen. "The Newly Minted MLS: What Do We Need to Know Today?" *Searcher*, May 1998. 30 April 2002 (http://www.infotoday.com/searcher/may98/story1.htm).

2. White, Herbert. *Quo Vadis – Librarianship? Opportunities and Dangers as We Face the New Millennium.* Englewood, CO: Libraries Unlimited, Inc., 2000: 321.

Chapter 8

Administration and Management

> *"A library vendor is not quite as reliable as a good used car salesman. At least with the used car salesman you can go somewhere else next time. With a vendor, your best quality is that latent streak of masochism that almost all systems librarians seem to develop on the job."*
>
> —Earl Lee[1]

Systems personnel in libraries often find themselves acting in an unofficial administrative capacity, as administrators with little technical knowledge must involve their IT departments in planning and managing large technology projects. All computer services librarians therefore need to understand the basics of project management and administration and must be prepared to assume responsibility for the direction of technology in their library, whether or not they have technically been hired in an administrative role. This is especially important when your institution becomes involved in a major endeavor such as an automation system migration project, but administration and management skills will also be needed in such everyday tasks as negotiating a service contract for your library's printers. You also will likely be involved with the library's administration in either writing technology grants or implementing grant-funded projects. (While the process of writing grants is beyond the scope of this chapter, there are a number of titles on grant-writing and library fund-raising that can assist you if you do take on such a responsibility.)

In larger institutions, systems librarians may also be lucky enough (depending on your perspective!) to manage their own staff. The skills required to manage people are significantly different than those necessary in managing technology, and managing nonlibrarian IT staff presents its own set of challenges. This is another situation in which your people skills and common sense will be as important—if not more so—as your technical knowledge. As Mark Stover writes: "People skills are critical for information technology managers because their first allegiance is to human beings, not computers. True, they will be working with computers every day, but only in the context of working with the *people* who use those computers."[2]

The tasks of technology project management and people management, while requiring distinct skill sets, each involve a great deal of planning and care to achieve properly. In the following sections, you'll find discussions of the skill sets needed in systems administration and management, as well as descriptions of what you might expect to encounter and the steps you need to take in completing common projects such as integrated library system (ILS) migrations and software rollouts. Begin with information on creating a technology plan, which is a necessary prerequisite to a number of large technology projects in libraries.

Creating a Technology Plan

Many libraries are required to create and submit a technology plan (usually covering a one- to five-year period) in order to satisfy state, board, or grant requirements. Technology plans are commonly required to receive E-rate discounts and state per-capita equalization grants, for example. While in the not-so-recent past only larger libraries tended to create such plans, smaller and medium-size institutions are now recognizing that managing the pace of technological change demands a more formal planning process. If you are required to create or contribute toward a technology plan for a particular purpose, be sure to review the specific guidelines of the body requiring the plan. If your technology plan is for the use of your library staff or administration rather than for a granting body or for your state library, keep your audience in mind; a major role for your document in this instance will be to provide the necessary information for others in your library to make informed technology decisions and use technology effectively in your institution.

The basic purpose of a technology plan is to state the library's mission and goals/objectives, then to explain how the library will use technology to fulfill those goals and objectives in terms of its mission. Your plan will need to include specifics on what you intend to do (with costs). Realize that your plan is not a "wish list" describing the technology you would ideally like to have but a statement of what your library truly intends to do with technology in the foreseeable future. Depending on the size and nature of your institution, you may hold the entire responsibility for developing your plan, may write it in conjunction with your director, may be the liaison to a planning consultant, or may be the technical liaison to or head of a technology planning committee composed of yourself and several other staff members. In any of these situations, however, the basic components and purpose of your plan remain the same.

Most technology plans contain several fairly standard sections. As you look through these, note how the earlier organizational and training tasks you have mastered in previous chapters will be useful in addressing these components. The standard areas of a technology plan are:

- *Introduction.* This brief section contains information on your library and on the plan's development, who was involved in its creation, and how it will be updated as needed.

- *Vision Statement.* Keep this short and to the point, showing how technology will help the library meet its goals in terms of serving its community over the next few years.

- *Background Statement.* You will need to build a foundation showing how technology has developed in your library, what technology you now own, and how it is currently used. This will be a much lengthier section and can include topics such as the way technology is integrated and used in general library functions, how much of the library's budget is allocated to technology, how staff and patrons use technology in the library, and the strengths and weaknesses of the library's existing technological environment.

- *Goals and Objectives.* This section lists and prioritizes major institutional goals that will be accomplished through the use of technology. Objectives describe the specific way in which you will implement technology to accomplish these goals.

- *Funding.* How will the library fund these goals? What percentage of funding will come from the library's own budget, and what percentage is anticipated to come from grants or other outside sources?

- *Training.* How are staff and patrons currently trained to use technology, and how will they be trained to use the new technologies you plan to implement? This can also include an evaluation of the skills of your current systems staff and a list of areas in which they might need to take classes or otherwise increase their expertise.

- *Evaluation.* Many plans will require you to describe how you will evaluate whether your goals and objectives are implemented within a given timeframe. You also may need to include a section on how often you intend to update your technology plan.

- *Conclusion.* This is optional for most technology plans and just wraps up the library's intentions.

- *Appendixes.* These optional sections can include library-created technology-related documents, such as handouts or class outlines.

If your library has created a technology plan in the past, you may merely be required to update it in terms of your current technological environment and needs. However, as many plans are updated only every three to five years, you may find that the older plan has outlived its usefulness or has failed to predict the current technological environment. In this case, you may be better off starting from scratch.

A useful list of resources related to technology planning, broken down by state, is accessible online at http://web.syr.edu/~jryan/infopro/techplan.html. This guide includes links to specific planning guides from state libraries, sample plans, grants and funding opportunities that require a technology plan, and other planning resources and guides. You can find additional sample plans and guides at *Integrated Library Systems Reports'* Web site at http://www.ilsr.com/tech.htm. Also consult Diane Mayo and Sandra Nelson's *Wired for the Future: Developing Your Library Technology Plan* (Chicago: ALA Editions, 1999). This title includes a number of checklists and worksheets to facilitate your planning process.

Creating your technology plan will also be a test of how well you (and/or your department) can work with the library's administration. Since technology is now so tightly interwoven with all library functions, planning for the future of technology means planning for the future of the library itself. Dealing with the bureaucracy of creating a technology plan and applying for programs such as the E-rate that require such a plan can be frustrating, partly because this removes you from the hands-on part of managing library technology and puts you smack into the middle of a bureaucratic muddle. As Tom Edelblute, public access systems coordinator at the Anaheim Public Library, notes, "I have not mentioned anything yet about dealing with library administration and government bureaucracy. There is a joke that an elephant is a mouse built to government specifications. When dealing with government programs like E-rate, this becomes readily apparent. There is a constant mess of forms and paperwork with grants, applications, and follow-up reports that can make you wonder why you took this job. For this your writing and presentation skills have to be good. As long as the end results of everything you do is appreciated by others you can sleep very secure at night. When it isn't, then it is time to move on."

Remember, however, that a willingness to work at overcoming bureaucracy and politics is necessary to doing your job effectively. Part of any systems librarian's administrative tasks will be to argue for increased shares of institutional funding and to allocate scarce resources in the most effective manner. Ensuring that technology serves the needs of the institution requires finding the funding to support technology. Working on a technology plan merely highlights this process. As another survey respondent wishes he'd learned earlier: "People skills, specifically being a politician. Everyone's so busy trying to teach you to be a decent librarian and the systems skills, no one ever mentioned how much being the systems admin is about political maneuvering."

Ensure that your technology plan is sensible and reflects the realities of time, goals, and funding at your institution. If you have historically had funding to replace computer equipment only every five years, for example, it does little good to describe your library as being on a more ideal three-year replacement cycle. (It would be better in this case to describe the reality of the situation and to use your technology plan to show the necessity for increased funding so that you could move to a shorter replacement cycle.) The process of creating a technology plan presents an opportunity for you to learn how to market yourself and your department and to show the importance of allocating funding to technology in order to fulfill the library's mission and goals. Take advantage of that opportunity!

Planning IT Projects

Whether or not you are officially in an administrative position, your technological expertise will be called upon when your library undertakes a large-scale IT project such as migrating to a new automation system or rolling out new software. The projects highlighted below are merely examples of the sorts of endeavors you are likely to be involved with; specific details and projects will vary depending on your environment and your institution's needs. In any IT venture, however, the focus needs to remain on completing the project with a minimum of disruption and with maximum benefit to the library's users and staff. Here, it might be useful to shore up on the basics of IT project management. The following sections will outline several common IT projects, beginning with (and most extensively discussing) the process of migrating to a new automation system. Although more complex than many projects you will need to deal with, the migration process illustrates areas you must attend to in many IT situations, and thus provides something of a case study for other projects.

Integrated Library System Migration

Most libraries are now automated, so you will be more likely to be called upon to plan the migration of your data to a new automation system than to automate from scratch (although much of this discussion will also be applicable to setting up a new integrated library system [ILS] as well). Many automation systems are nearing the end of their usable life, partially because they were intended largely to handle print resources and now need to manage access to resources and databases in a number of formats, while also meeting the rising expectations of users who may be comparing your systems to graphical, customized Web sites such as Amazon.com. Unfortunately, data migration presents its own set of pitfalls. Systems staff will need to work with technical and circulation services librarians to clean up data prior to the migration. Some data will inevitably be lost or corrupted in the changeover. The change in interface and functionality will be disruptive to library staff and users who have been accustomed to the old system. Computer hardware, networking, and operating systems may need to be upgraded prior to the migration.

You may also be called upon to work with your administration to set a timetable for migration. When doing so, consider all of the aspects in the following sections and create a realistic timeframe for changing your system over—then add several months. Realize that the only surety in migrating your automation system is that things will never go entirely as planned. There is no way around it: an automation migration will be time-consuming, disruptive, frustrating, and costly. Your job will be to plan carefully so that the changeover occurs with the minimum possible cost, disruption, and frustration. You may also be called upon to work with an automation consultant, if your institution/consortium chooses to use one—another instance in which your technical communication skills will come in handy.

Migrating an ILS successfully calls for different skills than those required in its day-to-day operation. The understanding of your particular automation environment that you have gained from maintaining it on a daily basis, however, will serve you well as you plan the migration of your data and the post-migration environment.

An Interview with Library Integrated Network Consortium (LINC) Manager Carol Dawe (January 2002)

Please give some background on your consortium, such as its size and its current automation environment.

- 8 public libraries within a 30-mile radius in the western suburbs of Chicago, Illinois

- 2.5 million in circulation in FY2001

- 478,500 bibliographic records

- 283,000 authority records

- 1,025,000 item records

- 150,000 patron records

We are a DRA/SIRSI library. We are running DRA Classic and DRA Web2. Currently we are looking at other vendors in order to migrate to a full Windows-based product. We have three NT servers and a Compaq Alpha 4100. We also provide Web hosting for seven out of the eight sites and a few community sites as well. We also have a mail server and provide e-mail for our members.

We have point-to-point T-1s linking each site to the central site and 2 Internet T-1s that go directly to a point of presence in Chicago. We have LANs at all sites and six out of eight are on Windows 2000. We have a WAN that connects the central site to each site. A firewall protects the central site and other security measures are also in place.

Please summarize the automation migration project that you're currently involved with.

SIRSI's purchase of DRA has completely shaken up the library automation industry as a whole and our consortium is feeling the effects of the decision to kill the TAOS product. Originally we had planned to look at SIRSI, Innovative Interfaces, and DRA's TAOS. With TAOS gone, we will look at Epixtech as well. Demonstrations will be held in February and then the various task forces within the consortium and the administrators will visit other sites and, with hope, a decision can be made by May and contracts ready by June. We will review our timetable at each monthly administrative council meeting.

What timetable are you using, and what major tasks need to be completed during the migration process?

We hope to migrate in October or November 2002, but we may slow the process down if we don't find a suitable vendor. We will review the timetable monthly. The rest is as I described earlier. Once contracts are signed, training and other migration issues will be pursued with help from the vendor.

What have you found to be the most important questions to ask a potential automation vendor?

- How hands-on will they be in the conversion process? This really is key.

- We have them describe their technical support.

- We have them describe their upgrading and release process.

- We have them describe their troubleshooting process.

What are the most important things to look for in choosing a new automation system?

New code. We want a product that will work well into the 21st century and not an old product that has been rewritten.

Potential is important. If the product is "done" then it isn't worth it.

Reliable technical support. It has to be a good fit. The products are all about the same. They just do things differently but the support is essential.

Please talk a little bit about database cleanup. What types of problems have you found that need to be checked and fixed to ensure the integrity of your data in the migration?

We are cleaning up our level S records, which are old records from CLSI. We also need to convert our serial records. They are still in monograph form. We have a lot of local practices in terms of authority work and subject headings that will also pose some problems.

What kind of training do you plan to provide to member library staff in preparation for the changeover?

It is going to vary quite a bit. I envision going to each library for circulation training and using a test database. We will train trainers and work with them, but LINC staff will be involved in each training session. We will train slow learners separately from the "experts" and more advanced staff members. It is going to be a real challenge and I'm looking forward to it.

What are member libraries in your consortium doing (in terms of upgrading systems, publicity, etc.) to help smooth the way for a successful migration?

I mentioned that in the first question. We are trying to get all eight libraries on a Windows 2000 platform. We are imaging workstations so that they are all the same and there is consistency.

What one piece of advice would you give to systems librarians involved in planning an automation migration?

As a friend of mine says: "Plan the work and work the plan," but also know that the plan can and will change. Be flexible when working with a vendor and consistent when working with your members. Keep the line of communication open and then everyone will be aware of the process and the various steps to be taken.

Is there anything else about planning a successful migration project that hasn't been addressed here?

Staff time concerns me. We are a staff of three full-time and three part-time. Will we be able to do all of this? That is why planning is so important.

Your level of direct involvement in your library's ILS migration project will vary, depending on your institutional needs and situation. If your library is part of a larger system or consortium, for example, many of the tasks below may be handled by staff at your system headquarters. In this case, however, you will likely be called upon to serve as your library's liaison to the larger system and to handle or coordinate details such as training and hardware upgrades within your own institution. You will also be required to attend vendor demos and to give input on the new system's desired capabilities and services.

Selecting a Vendor

In planning a migration project, your institution will first need to select an ILS vendor and product. The first step in choosing a vendor is to prepare a request for proposal (RFP). The basic purpose of an RFP is to outline your institution's automation needs and solicit vendor proposals that describe how their products and services can fulfill those needs. Writing an RFP has the added benefit of helping to clarify your library's automation requirements, as you will need to create a detailed analysis of such requirements in order to provide clear instructions to the responding vendors.

A number of sample RFPs and guides to creating an effective RFP are available online at http://www.ilsr.com/sample.htm. When examining others' RFPs, try to find samples from libraries that are similar to your own institution in scope and community served. Also consult the resources listed later in this chapter and in Appendix B to find more on the beginning stages of planning an ILS migration.

Your department may be tempted to choose an automation system by fiat, since one maxim of vendor selection is that you will never have complete agreement among library staff. Departments and individuals may tend to focus on a particular favored aspect or function—which may be purely cosmetic—and favor a system based solely on that aspect. However, you will need to work with library staff to ascertain the true needs of their department and to see how vendors can meet those needs. Systems librarians are responsible for looking at the entire picture and must work with their administration (and/or system/consortium) to select the vendor that will best meet the overall needs of the institution. This includes your need for affordable and useful vendor support and training, which is not always apparent from a demonstration. Vendor selection is often discussed on mailing lists such as SYSLIB-L; search its archives to find information on others' experience with the technology and the migration and technical support available from various vendors.

When researching a vendor, also keep in mind the needs of your library's patrons. The public access catalog is the library's online face to its users and needs to contain sufficient functionality and usability to satisfy your patron base. Realize that patron expectations are higher and ever-growing, as users accustomed to using the World Wide Web as a common graphical interface to a huge variety of information can be less than patient with text- and menu-based systems; with slowdowns and perceptible lag times; with needing to come to the library to use the OPAC, request an item, or read an article; and with using different databases for different purposes. Since newer OPACs are largely Web based, the vendors you are evaluating should be able to point you to sites that are using the latest versions of their products. Be sure to test the usability and usefulness of the public interface in a live environment.

Try to plan ahead. Since technology changes so rapidly, this is easier said than done, but take some time to try to foresee your library's future needs. Will you be cataloging Internet resources? Wanting to add the capability to simultaneously search multiple electronic databases and/or other libraries' systems through your ILS? Looking to add the ability to browse the OPAC through mobile devices such as PDAs? Adding book jacket images, patron reviews, tables of contents, and personalization features to the OPAC? Allowing patron-placed reserves and other self-service features? Moving to thin client technology? Will your system be undertaking large new building projects and dramatically expanding collections? Will your consortium be adding new members? What operating systems do you intend to support? Will you be looking for Internet or PC time-management software integration with your patron database? Do you wish to access local history resources or other local databases through the OPAC? Provide remote authentication? Add news and local information? Are you adding e-books? The answers to questions such as these can dramatically impact your choice of vendor. (There is insufficient space to address these questions thoroughly here, but see the Resources section and Appendix B for reading suggestions that include thoughts on how these elements can be integrated into an RFP.) If you are a smaller institution with less technical support available, you might also wish to investigate application service provider (ASP) options, in which your ILS is outsourced and hosted at the vendor's site.

Keep all of these factors in mind when composing your RFP, which must accurately reflect both your library's current automation environment and its future needs. Your systems inventory will be useful here in describing your current technological environment, as will statistics on your circulation, number of volumes, number of patrons, and so on. (This is a major reason for accurate record keeping!) Also consult your technology plan and try to integrate its goals with those of your automation RFP. Since an ILS is such a major part of library technology, choosing the right vendor is an important step in reaching those goals.

Open Source Automation Systems

Implementing a library automation system has historically been both costly and complicated. Furthermore, once your library has locked in a particular vendor's product, it can be even more costly and complicated to switch to a new supplier. A number of libraries have become dissatisfied with reliance on outside vendors and on expensive, proprietary systems. Enter the open source movement, which has begun to produce usable automation systems as an alternative to the large library vendors. (For more on open source, see Chapter 2.)

Open source automation systems are currently either in the early stages of development or more suitable for a smaller library environment, but many of the more promising projects bear watching as additional modules, stability, and functionality are added. To keep an eye on their development, see:

- *Avanti*: http://www.nslsilus.org/~schlumpf/avanti

- *Koha*: http://www.koha.org

- *Learning Access ILS*: http://www.learningaccess.org/website/techdev/ils.php

- *OpenOPAC*: http://openopac.sourceforge.net

- *Open Source Digital Library System Project*: http://osdls.library.arizona.edu

- *PhpMyLibrary*: http://phpmylibrary.sourceforge.net

The tremendous complexity of integrated library systems makes creating a viable one a particularly challenging task for the open source community, but the above projects may be worth examining as you prepare to switch vendors.

Also, even if an entire open source solution is inappropriate for your library's needs, you may wish to be on the lookout for open source tools that can extend the functionality of your ILS. Larger university libraries with a large systems staff, for example, have been able to devote resources to creating add-ons to the systems of a number of major vendors, and many are making these tools freely available to the library community as a whole. Follow the discussions at oss4lib, at user group meetings, and on your vendor's e-mail discussion list for ideas on how you might use these add-ons in your own library.

Lastly, if you wish to investigate open source alternatives to proprietary automation systems, be prepared to counter arguments about your library's past experience with "homegrown" solutions. Open source tools and techniques have matured greatly since the 1980s, which is the last time there was a major push to develop in-house automation systems, and the Internet has created an avenue for near-instantaneous communication that allows developers to share ideas and act on feedback in a way that was simply not possible in the past. Be

sure to amass current information and examples to coun-
teract your administration's memories of the costs and
stresses involved in the past; remember, institutions have
long memories.

Once you have received responses to your RFP, you will wish to
select the top bids. This is a decision that will involve you, your
administration, your consortium (if applicable), and possibly your
library's department heads. Decide on two or three vendors that
best meet the requirements outlined in your RFP. Then, invite
them out to demonstrate their systems. Be sure at least to have systems staff, administrators, and all department heads attend these
demos (nontechnical department heads may wish to attend just a
general overview and the demo of the module they will be working
with directly). Allow everyone direct input into selecting the best
vendor, and encourage them to ask questions of the vendor's representatives to help determine how these products can best meet
their needs.

After you have selected a vendor, you will need to contract with
that vendor for the migration of your data and for continuing support post-migration. Your contract should at the minimum include
a system implementation plan (with target dates), describe system
and operating costs, describe precisely what will be provided by
the vendor, and provide for ongoing service, technical support,
and security. If you wish the vendor to provide staff training,
include this in the contract as well. Involve your institution's
lawyer in this stage.

Data Cleanup

Once you have selected and contracted with a vendor, you will need to begin the migration process. The first step is to undertake a massive cleanup of your existing databases. "Clean" data will migrate much more smoothly than dirty, and if your institution has been using a particular system for some time, it is likely that you will have quite a bit of data to clean up. This will also be a good time to undertake that large-scale weeding or inventory project you may have been putting off; why pay to migrate records for missing items or those you are going to withdraw? By the same token, this will also be a good time to undertake a similar cleanup of patron records; why migrate patrons who have not owned a card or used your library in the past 10 years? You may also wish to upgrade locally created or sparse catalog records to full versions.

Although in most institutions the cataloging department will be doing the actual cleanup of records, systems personnel will likely be called upon to create reports for catalogers to work from and to be the liaison to the new vendor. This is another instance in which those library school cataloging classes will come in handy: An understanding of the MARC format will be useful here.

Types of database records that need to be deleted and/or upgraded in the cleanup include:

- Unlinked item records (with no attached bibliographic records or holdings)

- Bibliographic records with no holdings or items

- Records with "withdrawn" (or similar status) that need to be fixed/deleted before migration

- 856 links that don't go anywhere

- Unlinked and duplicate authority records

- Unauthorized headings (subject, name, title, name/title)

- Duplicate bibliographic records
- "See" references with linked bibliographic records

You will also need to replace nonstandard barcodes and will wish to upgrade older records that may not be in full MARC format.

Staff Training

Automation vendors generally provide some staff training as part of their migration package. Especially in larger institutions or consortia, however, not all staff will be able to attend vendor-sponsored training, which can be prohibitively expensive and limited in the number of people who can attend. It is essential, therefore, to include training in your migration plan. (For more tips on technology training in general, see Chapter 6.) If you have a staff of existing trainers, deploy them to each department to provide individualized training on the appropriate modules. If you do not, you may wish to conduct some "train the trainer" sessions, or have your vendor do so, and send people back to do the initial training of others in their departments.

Remember that changing ILS vendors will be nearly as traumatic for many staff members as was the library's initial automation, as they have had years to develop a workflow and perfect their command of the old interface. Keeping staff involved through the planning process will help ease the trauma, as informed and involved individuals are less likely to fear change than when it is seemingly imposed randomly from above. Focus on the positives that the new system will bring, and on any anticipated relief to workload and on built-in solutions to the often-clunky workarounds staff members have developed to bypass the idiosyncrasies of older automation systems.

Be sure to provide several rounds of training so that all staff have a chance to attend. Formal training needs to occur as close as possible to the actual changeover date to minimize the chance of staff forgetting all they have learned without an opportunity for hands-on practice. Allow sufficient time to practice on the training days, as well, as staff will only learn by doing. It will also be useful to close for a day or two post-migration to allow training in a live environment without the pressure of serving library patrons with the new software. Make sure that trainers are available during these days to answer questions and to provide refresher training as needed.

It may be useful to revisit the staff competencies you created in Chapter 2 and update them to reflect the library's new automation environment. Specific tasks and techniques will change, and providing staff with a list of competencies and the opportunity for self-assessment will allow you to see where additional training may be needed post-migration.

Computer Upgrades

When migrating to a new vendor, especially when moving from an older text-based automation system to a Windows/GUI interface, you first may need to upgrade computer hardware and operating systems to handle the new modules. If you have been using Windows 98 for your staff machines, for example, you may be required to upgrade to Windows 2000 (with consequent requirements for upgrading your hardware to support a more demanding OS). If you are housing the databases at your own institution or system, you will likely need to invest in a newer, more powerful server.

You may also need to examine your networking infrastructure to see if it can handle the demands of your new system. If you have been making do with a patched-together network, now is the time to measure your throughput and ensure that you have the bandwidth and network quality to support your requirements. The quality of the underlying network and its capacity to pass through a great deal of data becomes important.

Changing Over

The actual changeover process will stretch out over months, as all of the above tasks need to be completed prior to migration. Before migrating, you will also need to create policy files and work out security settings so that your cataloging and circulation departments can function effectively post-changeover. This is another time when a library background, especially in cataloging, will be useful. As Caryl Nemajovsky, systems librarian at Darton College, states: "I had to set up the library settings for our automation system when we transferred over. Unless I had some major library experience in all areas, without the degree I couldn't have done a very good job ... without knowing cataloging it would have been difficult to set up the proper initialization files, preferences, and security settings so the catalogers can do their work."

The actual changeover itself needs to be scheduled and planned months beforehand. If you have a large amount of data to migrate, or if you wish to provide staff training on a live system, you may wish to close your library for one or two days during the changeover to provide sufficient time for transition and training.

Patron Training

After any migration that affects the public face of your automation system, you will be required to provide training for your library's patrons on using the new system. This is especially important if you are changing from a text-based OPAC to a Web-based one, or in any situation where the patron interface changes dramatically.

Since it can be difficult to get patrons to attend training sessions, also be sure to provide detailed "cheat sheets" on using the new system. Have these available as handouts next to each patron terminal, and consider posting instructions on your Web site. Although your OPAC will have built-in help files, these can be lengthy and confusing for users who just want to get up and running. You might also make your own online instructions available via the catalog. (For a fun and unusual approach to getting patrons to learn to use the online catalog, see the Salt Lake County Library System's "Escape From the Library Mansion" game at http://www.slco.lib. ut.us/library_mansion/index.htm.) As Sandy Schulman suggests: "If you know that the instructions provided by the system vendor are unclear, rewrite them as soon as possible. I know you don't have the time, but believe me, it will take less time to write clear instructions than to have to help each individual user who runs smack into a riddle of instructions or tutorials from your vendor."[3] Also make sure that public service staff, assistants, and/or student workers in public areas are prepared to do informal patron training on system features.

Usability Testing

Although the underlying functionality of the public-access catalog is out of your control, many aspects of the patron's interaction with the catalog will be changeable. Most modern OPACs now use a Web-based interface; do not be afraid to tweak its settings. Change colors, change the appearance of buttons, change layouts, change defaults, and try to create the best and most usable interface for your patrons and staff. Before launching the new OPAC, install it on a test server and allow staff to have input into its usability and appearance, including that of the online help screens. You can also set up patron focus groups to give input on the new system from a typical user's perspective.

Resources

You are not the first librarian to feel the pain of planning an automation project, and there are a number of guides, articles, and online resources to assist you throughout the process. Just a few selected resources are listed below; find additional suggestions in Appendix B. Supplement these suggestions with your own research to find the most current guides before beginning your own migration project. You should also join and read your selected vendor's e-mail discussion list and/or online forums to gather pointers from other institutions using the same software.

- Barry, Jeff. "Closing In On Content." *Library Journal*, 2001. Accessible online: http://libraryjournal.reviewnews.com/ index.asp?layout=articleArchive&articleId=CA74708 This annual article surveys the automation marketplace over the past year and profiles a number of major vendors. A good starting point for locating vendor Web sites and getting an overview of capabilities; also includes helpful tables on sales to consortia, types of libraries using the system, and total numbers of installations.

- Cibbarelli, Pamela, ed. *Directory of Library Automation Software, Systems, and Services, 2002–2003*. Medford, NJ: Information Today, Inc., 2002. $89.00 This biannual reference source for library automation includes comparative information on software packages, automation consultants, retrospective conversion products, Internet resources, and conferences.

- Cohn, John M., Ann L. Kelsey, and Keith Michael Fiels. *Planning for Integrated Systems and Technologies: A How-To-Do-It Manual for Librarians*. New York: Neal-Schuman, 2001. $55.00 From RFPs to testing, a useful and practical guide that includes step-by-step coverage of all aspects of choosing and using an automation system.

- Doering, William. "Managing the Transition to a New Library Catalog: Tips for Smooth Sailing." *Computers in Libraries* 20(7), July/August 2000. Accessible online: http://www.infotoday.com/cilmag/jul00/doering.htm A veteran of three automation migrations shares his thoughts on creating a successful changeover, from training to timetables to communicating with vendors.

- *Integrated Library Systems Reports*: www.ilsr.com
  Articles and reviews, white papers, sample RFPs, vendor
  directory, press releases, and more.

- LibraryHQ's Library Automation Consultants: http://www.
  libraryhq.com/consultants.html
  A brief consultant directory, with links to consultant Web
  sites when available.

Software Rollouts

As with ILS migrations, the conversion to or addition of new
software packages can also be an extended process, encompassing
aspects such as the selection of appropriate software for your institution's needs, upgrading or replacement of outdated hardware
that may not run the new packages effectively, software installation, and staff and/or patron training. You may choose to roll out
new software gradually to give people a chance to get used to using
it before everyone needs to make the change.

Remember from Chapter 1 the importance of communication
in the work of any systems librarian. One reason that library staff
members are often resistant to changing technology is that they
were not involved in the decision-making process, and it therefore
appears that their computing environment shifted arbitrarily, with
no advance notice. As Mark Stover writes: "People are mystified
when they are expected to use a particular software application
and are clueless about its functionality. People are mystified when
changes appear in their computer systems (operating system,
desktop, applications, hardware, etc.) without any advance notice.
A good wired manager will prevent his or her employees from
becoming mystified."[4] Demystify the process by giving people
plenty of warning that the software environment will be changing.
Explain why it is changing. Provide training on the upgraded or
new program and the opportunity to practice with it. Ensure that
staff know who they can turn to for help with the new product.

Network Upgrades

Upgrading a computer network, another major and common undertaking, requires attention to similar details as do other IT projects. A network that is created and extended without proper planning can cause problems down the line, as connectivity and throughput become insufficient to support newer operating systems or the client modules of a new ILS, for example. While upgrading a network can be costly, this is a project for which grant money is often available. E-rate funds, for example, can be used for cabling as well as connectivity, and many state libraries offer technology grant money specifically for upgrading networks.

Decisions to be made here include:

- The type of cabling to use. Should you invest in fiber? Cat 5E? Cat 6? Wireless? Pricing, ease of installation, and institutional needs will affect your choice.

- Where and how to configure wiring centers. This will depend largely on the size and layout of your institution and on the cabling you choose to use.

- How much future expansion to allow for. Realize that any networking solution quickly becomes insufficient or obsolete; plan to be able to support many more network nodes than you currently intend to offer.

- The types of hardware and software upgrades that are needed. Are you upgrading your entire network to Windows 2000? Are you changing over to Linux? Do you need to invest in new servers, additional storage, additional RAM?

The decisions you make here will determine the scope and expense of your networking project and can help you also decide the extent to which you will need to involve outside consultants or vendors.

Managing Systems Staff

In many larger libraries, systems responsibilities are split among several people. You may be the only librarian in charge of several computer technicians, or you may be a library systems administrator with the responsibility for managing other systems librarians in addition to library technology. This requires you to gain supervisory skills in addition to whatever technical knowledge you need to keep library systems running. Managing technical staff, furthermore, requires different skills than managing librarians; IT can truly have its own culture, which means you need to work to bring your department into line with the larger library culture. Your IT people may also lack the library background and values of other library staff, which can create a communications gap between them and non-IT personnel. Your job is to bridge that gap and to give your employees the skills they need to interact more effectively with librarians and support library technology.

As an IT manager, you may be responsible for managing diverse groups, from other librarians, to paraprofessional staff, to nonlibrarian IT professionals, to student workers—and even volunteers. Each of these groups brings a different outlook, skill set, and focus to systems work, and you may need to deal with them in different ways. Systems staff may be part time or full time, and there may be individuals you rarely see because they are responsible for covering the department on nights and weekends when you are not present.

Unfortunately, supervisory skills are not always taught in library schools, which focus more heavily on professional skills and theory rather than on the specific skills needed in managing people. Our background as members of a helper profession, furthermore, can cause us to be a bit too helpful when it comes to managing our employees. The patron is always right—but your staff may not be. Lastly, in most libraries, systems staff will be limited, and your duties will be a mix of hands-on and administrative, requiring you to add management expertise to your skills toolbox. As with the rest of systems work, responsibilities here tend to be additive; you will be a manager in addition to, rather than instead of, being a systems librarian.

Communicating

The same skills that serve you well as you are interacting with, training, and serving as liaison to library staff and users will be your foundation as a successful manager. The key to a smoothly running department is communication and clarity; the relationship you build with your employees is equally as important as those you build with your superiors and peers. As Richard Warman points out: "At the top of most employees' gripe lists are problems in communication—not understanding what is expected of them, feeling excluded from important information, working under people who give vague and confusing instructions. When employees see their superiors as their main roadblock to getting their jobs done, the culprits are likely to be irrational or incompetent instruction-givers."[5]

The health of your department—and its relationship with other library departments—depends on your ability to maximize communication among your staff, yourself, other library employees, and patrons. Involve your staff in departmental decisions and recognize the value of their input, while clearly explaining your own motivations and positions to them. Communicate the importance of sharing knowledge with other library staff, which might be difficult for purely technical employees who may feel it is easier and quicker to resolve issues on their own and underappreciate those without formal technical training. Explain these ideals in terms of the mission of the institution and try to pass on library values; your staff will appreciate being informed of the reasoning behind department policies and priorities. Technical staff can be especially sensitive to micromanagement and will appreciate the opportunity to extend themselves professionally. Your job will be to ensure that their actions serve library goals, and to outline their responsibilities so that they have a framework to work within. Admire and hire people who can work independently, but remember broader institutional needs.

Also draw on your own background with technology in communicating with your staff. Technical personnel have greater respect for those who can speak their language, and, even if you have a better grasp on the larger picture than on the details, your technical knowledge will allow you to understand your staff's perspective and better communicate the library's needs.

Hiring and Staffing

In a larger institution, part of your responsibility as a systems librarian will be to deploy your staff effectively and to hire the right mix of people and skills for the smooth running of technology in your library. Unfortunately, finding money for technology and money for sufficient staff is often a tradeoff in an era of fixed library budgets and insufficient funding. Here, again, you will need to become politically savvy and learn how to market your department and its services and argue for sufficient funding to take care of yourself and your staff.

You will also need to master the skills involved in finding and hiring people who are the right fit for your institution. When looking for new systems staff, remember the skills, attitude, outlook, and capacity to learn and grow that have been important to your own success—these will be equally important to your staff's success. Specific technical skills are useful, but they can always be learned. As Roy Tennant emphasizes in a list of useful personality traits for digital library staff: "The capacity to learn constantly and quickly. I cannot make this point strongly enough. It does not matter what they know now. Can they assess a new technology and what it may do (or not do) for your library? Can they stay up-to-date? Can they learn a new technology without formal training? If they can't, they will find it difficult to do the job."[6] The ability to learn new technologies and to grow on the job is paramount. Remember your own need to extend your skills; your staff has a similar need. Learn again to fight for training dollars. While it is important that anyone you hire has the ability to learn independently, sometimes formal training will be necessary. Training and the opportunity for professional growth also always rank high on IT personnel's wish lists, so providing such opportunities will help you retain staff in an environment where you will likely be unable to pay the most competitive salaries.

If you are in an academic library, you may be responsible for supervising student workers, who are intended to assist in troubleshooting, computer labs, and so on. Student workers may lack a commitment to the principles of librarianship and require more supervision than other staff, although they may possess a great deal of technical knowledge that can be harnessed to help fulfill the goals of your institution. Technical management here requires attention to the mix of employees and the optimal way to deploy them throughout the institution, which you will best learn through time and experimentation. The right staffing mix depends largely on the type and scope of technology implemented in your library, as well as the technological comfort level of other library staff.

As a systems manager, you will be responsible for interviewing, hiring, and evaluating your employees. In any interview, remember that you and the candidate are truly interviewing one another to see if the institution and the position will be a good match for the candidate's skills and personality. In any hiring process, search not only for technical skills, but also for the ability to work well in a library environment—which includes communication skills and the ability to empathize with the library's mission. Search for people with whom you and other library staff can work well and who will help you fit technology into the library environment. When reviewing your staff, evaluate them in terms of goals such as: Do they support technology within the library well? Do they understand the library environment and arrange their priorities accordingly? Do they interact well with library staff and users? Can they work independently?

In all, you are seeking staff who share or can learn a similar outlook to yours, one based on the principles of librarianship and that melds library skills with technological savvy. You will need to work together to ensure that library technology serves the needs of your institution's users.

Works Cited

1. Lee, Earl. *Libraries in the Age of Mediocrity*. Jefferson, NC: McFarland & Co., 1998: 9.

2. Stover, Mark. *Leading the Wired Organization: The Information Professional's Guide to Managing Technological Change*. New York: Neal-Schuman, 1999: 314.

3. Schulman, Sandy. "Applying a Proactive Ounce of Prevention." *Information Today*, July/August 1998: 46.

4. Stover, 91.

5. Warman, Richard Saul. *Information Anxiety 2*. Indianapolis: Que, 2002: 225.

6. Tennant, Roy. "The Most Important Management Decision: Hiring Staff for the New Millennium." *Library Journal*, February 15, 1998. 4 May 2002 (http://libraryjournal.reviewsnews.com/index.asp?layout=article Archive&articleId=CA156490). Tennant also notes the importance of flexibility and the ability to foster change among his list of useful traits.

Chapter 9

Life Lessons

> *"The sad fact is that many library bosses are also dysfunctional to one degree or another. You're lucky if your boss is simply neurotic as opposed to psychotic."*
>
> —Will Manley[1]

Classwork provides the necessary foundation, but only real-life experience can actually create a successful systems librarian and prepare you to be an effective negotiator for yourself and your career. The true pluses and minuses of systems librarianship become apparent as you settle into your profession, and each technology librarian must make a personal decision as to whether the rewards and opportunities outweigh the inherent frustrations. Many universities give credit for "life experience"—and for good reason! All of your experiences and interactions with library staff, patrons, and colleagues go into forming the foundation of your philosophy of systems librarianship, as well as the framework for your day-to-day activities.

While classwork is no substitute, advice from other professionals and an awareness of the potential pitfalls (and opportunities) will help you prepare to make the most out of your experience with systems-related work in libraries. In the following sections, find information on dealing with some real-world situations not covered in any class, including finding a job, moving into careers in related fields, negotiating a promotion, dealing with technostress, and the ethics of systems librarianship. Included are comments from working systems librarians who have themselves been there.

Finding a Job

Although most systems librarians initially enter their careers unintentionally, many choose to stay in the field, finding the challenges and opportunities of systems work personally rewarding. Having built up your technology skills in one library, you may wish at some point to seek a new systems position in another. You will be better able to locate opportunities and negotiate terms if you have first done your research on the types of positions available and if you are cognizant of the potential pitfalls of beginning a new library systems position. Having the facts will also be useful if you are considering becoming a systems librarian or if you currently work in a nonsystems position in a library but are considering changing specialties.

Finding a rewarding new position as a computer services librarian is a good news/bad news proposition. First, some good news: Systems-related jobs in libraries are relatively abundant. Libraries are in dire need of people with technical aptitude and a willingness to help manage technology, so it may be easier to find a job with this focus than one in another subfield of librarianship. Several survey respondents mention encountering a plethora of open positions, one noting that: "Certainly the pay is better, and the job opportunities more plentiful, for systems work as compared to 'traditional' library work."

While many systems librarians originally grew into their responsibilities at the time technical skills first became needed at their library, when they leave their institutions, they leave a hole that may take some time to fill. Incumbents will have had years to develop expertise with their library's particular technological environment—and to build its complexity. Most will be leaving behind an environment that has over the past few years evolved to require consistent systems support. This makes it much more difficult for an institution that has previously had a systems librarian in place to take the time to "grow" a replacement candidate from inside than for a library that has never had someone to manage its systems, which can build such complexity gradually. If you have built or learned technical skills yourself in previous positions (or in library school), you will be in a good spot to enter a position where a previous systems person has blazed the way.

The good news continues: Systems-related jobs in libraries tend to start with somewhat higher salaries than other positions in libraries. This, however, is relative; since systems jobs often also include responsibility for other library duties in departments from reference to technical services, and since they come with attendant stresses, systems librarians also earn their money. Many library administrations do, however, recognize the importance of compensating and retaining technically skilled staff, and salaries often reflect that understanding. This is particularly true if a position requires certifications or programming experience.

Academic libraries may prefer to hire librarians over non-MLS computer administrators for technical positions; at some institutions, librarians with faculty status can start at a higher pay scale than IT personnel in nonfaculty positions, increasing the odds of retention. Other libraries take the opposite tack, as Roy Tennant notes: "It's difficult to find librarians who are conversant with technology and who also are willing to work at the salaries we offer. In order to fill the jobs we have, some organizations have resorted to hiring tech-savvy librarians into a non-librarian classification—simply to offer better pay."[2] This is one reason for the diversity of job titles mentioned in Chapter 1, as individuals in similar positions may be classified quite differently, depending on the policies and pay scales of their parent institutions.

Systems-related jobs in libraries, however, do tend to have lower compensation than technology-related positions outside of libraries; the lower salaries endemic to librarianship carry through to technology positions. While computer-related work is generally more lucrative relative to other subfields of librarianship, salaries are still lower than those in many equivalent private sector IT jobs. We are all familiar with the tendency of female-dominated professions such as librarianship to have historically lower salaries than others requiring equivalent education and experience, and women in IT in general earn 12 percent less than men in comparable positions.[3]

Additionally, while librarianship has traditionally been seen as a lower-stress field, managing the systems that are essential to the library's operation and dealing with constant change can bring private sector stresses without bringing an equivalent level of compensation. Since most library operations are now dependent on the smooth functioning of computer technology, you may not view your position as lower-stress when, say, the network goes down and all eyes turn to you to resolve the situation. (Read more about technostress later in this chapter.)

But for many, the opportunities the library field offers more than offset these difficulties. As Bloomfield Township Public Library's systems department head Deb Downing mentions: "Even though family and friends suggest that the business world has much more to offer (i.e., compensation) for my skills and knowledge, I love working at libraries. There are many other rewards in libraries, and I do not plan to ever leave the library culture!" Systems jobs in public and academic libraries, furthermore, are more stable in uncertain economic times than are private sector IT jobs; you will likely never have to worry for the security of your position. Ben Ostrowsky, automation services technologist at the Tampa Bay Library Consortium, notes in his survey response that: "My friends thought I was crazy for not taking a dot-com job with lots of stock options. Our library consortium is going strong after over 20 years; they're dot-gone."

While you are absorbing this mixed news about the systems librarian job market, also realize that those writing the job ads for systems librarians may have only the vaguest idea of their library's true technology needs. This can unfortunately make it difficult for you to create an effective application for the position, can discourage applicants who do have the qualifications actually needed (rather than those listed in the ad), and will lead to surprises when you do start working. Try to ascertain during your interview the technological savvy of your immediate superior and the library's administration. See if you can talk with people who have worked with technology in the library in order to get an accurate overview of the existing computing environment. Some administrators may have an unfortunate tendency to pepper their job ads with buzzwords because they have heard that "X" product (or programming language, or software package) represents the latest and greatest in technology. Whether "X" serves the library's needs or actually represents its current technological environment remains to be discovered.

Also, note that job descriptions—especially technical job descriptions—often contain a "wish list" that describes the qualifications of the institution's *ideal* candidate. In the real world, administrators and search committees do not necessarily expect to find someone with every single skill and qualification listed in a particular ad. If you have some of the skills mentioned, and believe you could reasonably acquire the rest, or if you have related skills that could meet the library's needs, do not let a lengthy list of qualifications in a posting dissuade you from applying. One survey respondent suggests that you "... apply for systems jobs even if you think you are not qualified—you might be surprised." Be sure, however, that you are prepared to describe in your cover letter and in an interview how your existing skills can apply and how you intend to acquire additional knowledge in the desired areas.

Untangling the Job Ad

Deciphering position advertisements for technology librarians can be an art in itself. Some ads are unfortunately brief or vague, forcing you to make assumptions about an institution's technological environment and providing little help as you try to show how your qualifications match that library's needs. Other ads may seem to err on the side of verbosity, listing every possible qualification, software package, and skill. In academic environments, ads may have been written by committee, sometimes becoming an unfortunate amalgamation of personal preferences and institutional requirements.

When reading an ad, look first for any specific required or preferred technical qualifications. These usually take the form of statements like:

- Minimum five years experience managing and implementing integrated library systems

- Knowledge of Web programming and scripting languages

- Demonstrated knowledge of computers, networks, library automated systems, emerging technologies, and Windows operating systems

- Knowledge of networking, Internet, and software applications

Your own best defense against vague requirements such as the above is specificity. If the ad asks for "knowledge of networking," clarify in your cover letter and resume the type and size of network(s) you have administered. If it asks for "knowledge of Web scripting languages," provide the URL of a library Web site you have created and explain how you have used JavaScript, Perl, and/or other scripting tools to enhance its performance. Also, check the organization's own Web site to get a better sense of its computing environment—you should at least be able to ascertain the library's ILS vendor and the types of computing facilities available for patron use.

Ads that tend toward the overly specific will list requirements such as:

- Knowledge of Windows NT/2000 Server, Windows NT/2000 for workstations, Windows 98, IIS, Novell 4.0, Office 2000, DOS, OCLC CATMe, NOTIS, Ex Libris, ILLiad, Ariel, Procite, McAfee Antivirus, terminal emulator applications, Dell Inspiron troubleshooting, HTML, XML, Perl, Java, Javascript …

Respond to such kitchen sink ads by focusing on the major points and on your major strengths. Explain your skills and background in network administration, point to the URL of a Web site you have worked on, and describe your ILS and cataloging support activities. Emphasize your willingness to extend these skills to encompass the specific software packages used in the particular library's environment.

Forewarned is forearmed, and it is good to be aware of potential pitfalls before applying. Also be aware that in many institutions you will have broader responsibilities than those specific to maintaining library technology; you may also be required to work the reference desk, catalog materials, help develop the library's collection, and/or manage a circulation department. Scrutinize such split positions carefully to ensure that you will be able and willing to undertake all of their duties, and that the compensation is relatively fair for the activities required.

To maximize your chances of finding a position that is a "good fit," be sure to examine your potential working environment, and not only your potential salary. Remember that in dealing with your supervisor and coworkers, you will be dealing with them not only as a colleague but also as a representative of the library's computing environment. Consider carefully whether you wish to work in an institution where the staff seems fearful of or resistant to technology and to change. Be sure that you get to talk directly with your future supervisor and/or administrator during your interview, as these are the people whose support you will later need when it comes to arguing for important decisions regarding the library's computing environment. As one survey respondent emphasizes: "When you interview for a position, scrutinize the person who will be your supervisor very carefully. They should make it clear they support risk-taking, and provide guidance and mentoring to those they supervise. If they don't or if something concerns you about their behavior, don't take the job."

Beyond ascertaining the technological environment, level of support, and computing expertise at your new institution, also be aware of the opportunities your new position may (or may not) offer for professional development. While all librarians require professional development opportunities and support, this is doubly true for systems librarians, who need to keep current both in the library field and with new technological developments that will affect the computing environment in their institutions. Ask if the library provides funding to attend conferences, classes, and workshops; ask what former systems personnel have done to keep up their skills. While there are a number of low-cost alternatives available (see Chapter 7), sometimes there is no substitute for a formal class or conference.

Also think carefully about the size and type of library you are willing to work in. If you are comfortable with the thought of working independently and serving as a solo systems librarian, a smaller public library may be right for you. If you want the chance to be on the cutting edge of technology, or prefer to work as part of a larger systems staff, you may instead investigate options in larger, better-funded research institutions or large public library systems. If you do not wish to work with the public and prefer a more specialized environment, look at corporate opportunities. Think about whether you would prefer to specialize in one area of systems work, such as Web design, training, or network administration, or if you prefer to have responsibilities in a variety of areas. Your answers to these questions have a large influence on the types of positions you should be applying for.

If you are considering systems librarianship as a new career, it will also be useful to familiarize yourself with the field's ups and downs by speaking with working systems personnel in libraries before committing yourself to a job or a path of study. Follow the discussions on a mailing list such as SYSLIB-L, see if your library school has a mentoring or job shadowing program, and try to set up informational interviews with systems librarians at nearby libraries. (Note that an informational interview differs from a job interview. You are not necessarily seeking a position at that particular library; you are merely trying to get an inside look at the daily responsibilities of the job.) You will find that most librarians are eager to share their experiences and will be honest about both the pitfalls and the promise of dealing with technology in libraries. If you are currently enrolled or are planning to enroll in library school, try to locate an internship in the field. Real-world experience will give you the best indication of the true advantages and disadvantages of the specialty.

Once you are convinced that it is time to seek a systems position, note that job opportunities can be found in a number of different ways. Library technology associations such as LITA and ASIST hold free placement centers at their annual meetings; this can be a great way of focusing your search to technology-related positions in libraries and to attend in-person interviews with out-of-state institutions. Even if you cannot attend the meeting, you may be able to submit your resume for scrutiny by potential employers. Both associations also maintain online joblines (LITA's at http://www.lita.org/jobs and ASIST's at http://www.asis.org/ Jobline), which are good sources for information technology positions in libraries. Job ads are also often posted to SYSLIB-L and to other e-mail lists for systems librarians, so additional advantages accrue to those using online tools to stay connected. Lastly, do not forget to consult employment resources that are less specifically focused on technology, such as the general library journals (both in print and online), local library schools, and major library career-related Web sites such as Lisjobs.com (http://www.lisjobs.com) and Library Job Postings On the Internet (http://www.libraryjobpostings.org).

Branching Out

Work as a systems librarian will also prepare you for work in a number of other related fields. Many systems librarians move in and out of libraries or go on to choose to work for related industries such as library automation vendors and database companies. Skills learned on the job as a computer services librarian provide a useful background for positions as trainers, support representatives, metadata specialists, and product managers, each of which requires a unique mix of library and technical knowledge.

An Interview with Endeavor Information Systems, Inc. Corporate Recruiter Geri Hernandez (February 2002)

Please describe briefly the typical types of positions you hire for.

Endeavor looks for highly skilled technical people, candidates with three to five years of experience in a library environment or a combination of both, and sometimes we hire new grads. The highly technical candidates would fill our programming or development roles, while the experience of working in a library would come in handy when dealing with customers in a project management role or a training role, since the employee must understand where their customer is coming from or what the customers want. Graduates with MLS degrees usually fill our Customer Support roles since they understand the customers' issues and can gain a better understanding of our company and can grow into other positions within our company.

What background and skills are useful in these positions?

We look for people with an educational background that pertains to the library industry ... i.e., Masters in Library Science or an equivalent of five years of professional library experience. It is also advantageous if a candidate has had previous experience working with a particular integrated library software system, especially if it has been of a technical nature like tech support. Overall, library workflow knowledge is preferred and in some positions knowledge of MARC is mandatory. Candidates from an academic/higher education background seem to fit better than ... candidates from a public library.

What do librarians bring to certain jobs that those with a strictly technical background lack?

Librarians understand the needs of their colleagues, other librarians. Many times, employees with solely a technical background lack the skills to understand what librarians are looking for, need, or want in integrated library software. Librarians working for an ILS vendor usually possess the back office knowledge of a library necessary to accurately assess the needs or problems faced by the end-users or librarians.

What different demands does working as, say, an Endeavor trainer or product specialist place on your employees than those they would face in a library environment?

The daily demands of working in the profit sector are much different than the day-to-day demands on a librarian. The most significant difference is the pressure and inflexible deadlines of working for a profit sector vs. a nonprofit sector. The profit sector operates at a much faster and demanding pace. Often, librarians who first come into the profit sector usually underestimate the demands of the job.

What unique benefits does working for an automation vendor bring?

The ability to use your library knowledge, degree, and skills within the technology industry. Working for a vendor also has financial benefits.

What advice would you have for systems librarians who are considering branching out and working in related fields and industries (such as for ILS vendors)?

The best advice is to be really honest and realistic with their long-term career goals. Make sure they understand the demands that the position will require from them. Talk to others in the industry. Determine what they will need to sacrifice to be successful in the career they choose.

You also might consider contributing to the profession by writing on technical topics for library journals or publishers.

Recognizing the impact of computer technology and the need for librarians to learn about technological issues, many library-related publishing outlets are on the lookout for writers who can address computer-related topics from the library perspective. Information Today, Inc., for example, publishes a number of relevant journals (information available online at http://www.infotoday.com/periodicals.htm), and LITA and ASIST's member publications are always looking for content. If you have an idea for a monograph, Neal-Schuman and Information Today tend to publish large numbers of technology-related titles for librarians, while more general library publishing houses sometimes include technical topics among their offerings.

Also, general library journals often include technology-related articles. These journals may be a good outlet if you have a knack for clearly explaining technical issues to a general audience. Look for special opportunities to contribute to thematic issues such as *Library Journal/School Library Journal's* quarterly *netConnect* supplement, or propose a computer-related article that could benefit a majority of readers. Library publications often look for "how I did it in my institution" articles, which provide you with an opportunity to describe an innovative or particularly useful deployment of technology at your library. In any of these cases, both your library and your technical skills will be useful as you research and compose your manuscript. If you are in an academic institution, you may instead wish to submit work to peer-reviewed journals to assist in your quest for tenure or promotion. Applicable outlets here include publications such as LITA's *Information Technology and Libraries, MC Journal,* and *LIBRES,* as well as more general academic library journals.

Technology book reviewers are also in demand. Although library publications generally do not pay for book reviews, you do get to keep the copy of the book and will gain the advantage of having your name out as a technical expert. LITA's *Technology*

Electronic Reviews (http://www.lita.org/ter), for example, publishes reviews of library-related technology titles, and *Free Pint* (http://www.freepint.co.uk) reviews Web-related titles, while general library journals often include technology titles in their review sections. Lastly, consider serving as a referee for one of the technology-related peer-reviewed library journals, which occasionally will post calls for applicants on technology lists or in the journals themselves. Watch for calls for contributors, referees, and reviewers on your mailing lists and in journals you follow.

Negotiating a Promotion (or Raise!)

If you are willing and flexible enough to take on systems responsibilities as well as traditional library duties, or if multitasking appeals to you, adding systems duties to your normal tasks can be a good starting point for arguing for increased compensation and/or a promotion. You should especially consider brushing up on your negotiating and self-promotion skills if you are an accidental systems librarian who has already taken on these additional responsibilities without a concomitant increase in salary and change in job title. Research the job market to see what other professionals in similar positions are being offered, and be prepared to defend your request. As one survey respondent succinctly states: "Get more money than they are offering. You are probably worth more."

Be able to enumerate the benefits your work as a systems librarian brings to your institution. This will be most effective if you cite specifics. ("The new network has enabled staff to ..." "We have taught __ public Internet classes in 2002 ..." "Bringing support in-house has saved the library __ dollars this year.") Unfortunately, if you have been doing your job effectively, your contributions may seem invisible—as long as computer systems are running smoothly, your administration may not realize the potential for disaster without someone continually making the necessary adjustments to ensure they remain stable.

If you have taken advantage of opportunities to improve your technological skills through attending classes, earning certifications, or self-study, this can be another tool in your promotion arsenal. Traditionally, libraries have seen fit to provide pay increases and promotions for those who take charge of their own education and improve the service they are able to give the library by attending library school, earning an LTA certificate, and so on. Taking computer classes and earning certifications should be similarly rewarded, since you are learning practical skills in order to carry out the duties of your position more effectively.

If your attempts to gain increased compensation or recognition go unrewarded, be prepared to back up your arguments with action. Start looking for another job. You are responsible for managing your own career, and the market for experienced systems librarians is strong enough that you should have no problem making a move. The threat of losing you to another institution may shake your administration out of its complacency as it faces the possibility of having to attract and train a new systems person. Do not be surprised if they make a counteroffer. If not, you will likely be able to increase your salary by taking the time to find an appropriate position elsewhere; do not try this technique if you are not ready to walk. As *Information Week* notes about IT positions: "As much as companies vow to retain their best people, the reality is that it's a whole lot easier to get a pay hike from a job interview than a salary review."[4] This is as true in the library world as it is in corporations, and you have the added bonus that any slump in the corporate IT world is unlikely to affect the availability of positions in academic and public libraries. The plentiful nature of systems jobs in libraries gives you a stronger bargaining position, as your institution will realize that you can easily go elsewhere.

Realize also that merely being willing to fight for fair compensation, promotion, and recognition can have an impact on how you are perceived within your institution. Since much of effective systems librarianship involves being able to argue for the resources to do your job properly, you need to lay the foundation of respect that will make your administration take you seriously in future discussions. As Deborah Kolb and Ann Schaffner note: "... getting what you are worth is not just about money. It is about perceptions of your worth and your contribution. Your perception—and that of others—will affect your ability to command the resources and respect you need to do your job effectively. Each time you successfully negotiate the salary you deserve, you lay the groundwork to get the resources you need and you pave the way for others in the profession to do the same."[5]

Technostress

Although most people who gravitate to systems work in libraries tend to be more flexible and enthusiastic about change than is the norm, technostress still takes its toll. This is partially due to the additional level of responsibility library systems personnel assume in keeping themselves up-to-date with the latest technologies, and partially due to the frustrations inherent in trying to maintain computer systems and placate computer users when inevitable outages occur. A number of respondents to the accidental systems librarians survey mentioned inadequate time and resources as the most frustrating aspect of their jobs, and many also emphasized the difficulty in keeping up with new opportunities and technologies while continuing to keep current equipment and software running. Also note that while systems librarians do tend to enter the field accidentally and their beginning successes are lauded, these initial technological successes only raise the bar and increase their administration's expectations of future performance—even though future and additional systems may be more difficult and time-consuming to manage. Although systems increase in complexity and systems librarians' tasks increase over the years, this increased complexity will likely not be appreciated by library staff and administrators who just see either that things are humming along—or that they are not.

Technostress (especially when combined with the lower compensation endemic to library work) can also be a major factor in driving library systems people out of the field. As one survey respondent notes: "I don't get paid near enough extra money for this additional aspect of my job. I don't mind it much of the time, but I definitely don't intend to do systems work at any future job. I'd like it more if I could get more training and therefore more knowledge; but who has the time? I have access to a large group of online courses that would help me a lot, but it's all I can do to keep up with my job duties—I just can't find the time to take the courses."

Technostress often stems from physical causes, as well. Many libraries, especially smaller institutions, have added technology incrementally and ad hoc rather than planning it out, as when setting up a new building or lab. Such libraries often give short shrift to ergonomics issues and comfort factors, shoehorning equipment into existing furniture and fitting it where possible throughout the library. This affects all staff, but systems librarians are particularly vulnerable to problems such as carpal tunnel, eyestrain, and backache, due to the amount of time spent working with technology. Argue for attention to ergonomics, and do what you can to adjust your own environment. If you find yourself aching or developing tension headaches, take a break, stretch, walk around, and get out from behind the monitor. Just paying attention to your own physical well being can have a dramatic impact on how you feel about supporting library technology.

This discussion is not intended to warn you away from library systems work, but to raise your awareness of the stresses inherent in these types of positions. The lack of time to keep up with current technology or to provide an optimum level of support for library staff and users was mentioned by a large number of survey respondents. To be an effective systems librarian, you must be willing to commit to a path of lifelong learning—as well as to fight for the time and resources to back up that commitment. You must learn to value constructive change and to thrive on its presence.

Also be prepared to work with library staff and users who refuse to take responsibility for learning about technology. You can create training opportunities for such individuals (see Chapter 6), but you will find that a number are resistant to change to the extent that they refuse to learn and will call on you for every difficulty involving computers, even those problems that are easily resolved by an action as simple as rebooting the machine. This requires you to learn to manage and prioritize your own time. Most libraries lack the luxury of excess systems staff to hold users' hands, so try not to enable dependent behavior. One of the more frustrating aspects of systems work can be the constant interruptions from staff and users wanting an immediate resolution to an annoying (to them) yet minor problem, while you are attempting to find the time to work on a major project such as an ILS migration or technology plan. While you wish to encourage an open-door policy, you also need to maintain the ability to prioritize, and you must refrain from taking up all of your time solving problems that staff could easily resolve on their own.

This is a situation in which it will be helpful to plan for the education of your coworkers. Go back to the computer competencies you created in Chapter 1, and ensure that all library employees have the training and resources they need to achieve these competencies. If you are repeatedly interrupted with the same issue, create a "cheat sheet" for all relevant staff members that explains step-by-step how to resolve the situation. Insist that staff complete the steps on these handouts before you help them with these common problems, and establish as early as possible the tasks that you and other systems staff will not be responsible for (such as changing printer toner, removing paper jams, or rebooting a frozen terminal). While this may lead to grumbling on the part of some staff members, the savings to your time and sanity will more than balance out the impact of any dissension.

Any computer skills you can teach your coworkers or that they acquire on their own will go a long way toward helping technology in your library run more smoothly. Have no fear about educating yourself out of a job; remember, there is as much for you to learn as for them and your skill set is very different! As one survey respondent explains: "Don't be afraid to share knowledge and information with others. Knowledge does not necessarily equal power in this environment. You're better off teaching your colleagues how to do some things on their own."

Useful basic troubleshooting skills to teach your library's staff include:

- Rebooting a malfunctioning machine before calling technical support. (Be sure to teach staff that, if neither a proper shutdown nor Control-Alt-Delete will work, they can use the reset button, the off switch, or the power plug to power down the machine manually when needed.) When someone calls you for technical support, always ask whether they have rebooted before taking the time to go and investigate the problem in person.

- Using Control-Alt-Delete (at least on staff machines; this combination may be blocked by security software or network policies on patron systems) to shut down a frozen application.

- Trying to access a nonresponding Web site on a second machine before concluding that the problem is with a particular PC (rather than with the particular site).

- Clearing paper jams from, adding paper to, and changing the toner in laser printers.

- Checking to see if monitors, computers, and printers are securely plugged in—and connected to each other— before concluding that a system has died or will not boot.

Additional skills may be appropriate for your library's specific technological environment. Make sure also that staff have enough basic knowledge to accurately report a problem to systems personnel and to fill out the report sheets you created in Chapter 4. These skills are especially important for public service staff members, who will generally be the first to encounter problems with public-access workstations. Also make it clear what public-service staff will be expected to support—are they responsible, for example, for showing patrons how to use the features of Microsoft Word? Helping them send e-mail? Assisting them in pasting a resume into a form on the Internet? You will likely wish to emphasize supporting library-related functions such as the OPAC and subscription databases over helping users with incidental computer issues with features such as e-mail or chat. Ensure that non-systems staff know what they will be responsible for helping patrons with and what falls outside the scope of their duties. This will also help ensure a consistent environment for users, so they do not find that one day one staff member can help them and the next day a different staff member refuses to do so or does not know the software well enough.

You may find more acceptance if you make incremental changes to what library staff are expected to do. Allow them to build their skills and feel confident in each step before demanding more. Dramatically changing expectations all at once will trigger staff's fear of change and resentment at being handed additional tasks that may have been taken care of for them in the past, but empowering your colleagues bit by bit will increase their confidence in their own skills and result in their wanting to accomplish more on their own. Think of this as an evolutionary process of creating change; taking incremental steps over time can lead to dramatic results. As the change agent within your library, it is incumbent upon you to work to conquer your colleagues' fear of change. As Seth Godin writes: "We start by bypassing our fear of change by training people to make small, effortless changes all the time."[6] Dramatic, sudden change gives people something to talk about and to fear, while consciously making change a gradual process allows them to build their confidence with each step.

Staff will also be less resistant to change if they are kept informed of the changes before they happen, and of the reasoning behind any changes. Always keep the lines of communication open, and be aware of the potential for staff to see technology shifts as being imposed from "on high" with little rhyme or reason. Involve appropriate staff in technology decisions as much as possible, and show them how any change will positively impact the way they do their day-to-day tasks. Clark and Kalin note that: "What many regard as technostress is really resistance to change. Resistance is certainly not new, nor is it limited to computerization."[7] Make it your task to gradually reduce this resistance.

Sharing knowledge and building incremental change allows you to reduce the technostress level in other library staff members and yourself. The more others are able to do, the less basic technical support you will have to provide, freeing you up for other duties. The more they are able to do, the more they will feel empowered by technology rather than overwhelmed by it. Realize that neither stress nor technostress is a new phenomenon in libraries—although this may seem to provide little comfort to librarians overwhelmed by the perception of constant change, realizing the constancy of change can help you keep some perspective.

Ethics

Systems librarians tend to encounter stresses in other forms as well. While patron privacy and confidentiality have been cornerstones of the philosophy of librarianship, privacy and other ethical issues are compounded by the power of technology. Technological advances make it possible to collect information on the activities of patrons and library staff members that was previously unavailable, and much of this information may be automatically generated without any specific effort on the part of library systems personnel. For example, some personalized Web site and catalog services can have the side effect of allowing libraries to track individual usage patterns. Automated catalogs can keep transaction logs on library items. Web server logs can track visitors by IP address. You may be involved in deciding whether and how long to keep and whether to use or view this information, or in creating and posting privacy policies for your Internet services.

Given these technical possibilities, libraries should create policies on the collection and usage of electronic information. As pertains to staff, for example, staff members should be aware if the institution is collecting information on their e-mail usage and/or Web sites visited. Packages such as WebSense that have been implemented as filtering solutions in a number of libraries also have the ability to track where users have been by user name or by department. You and your administration need to decide whether such reporting will be implemented and how it will be used. This is an especially tricky issue for librarians who are part of a larger institution such as a university or a corporation, whose rules and philosophy might differ considerably from the library's perspective. As pertains to patrons, we have a responsibility to let our users know whether they have the same expectations to privacy of their electronic resource usage as they have had in the past for items such as circulation records.

These privacy issues also extend to internal technologies such as your local area network. If you have administrative privileges on the network, you also likely have the ability to view network-stored files and documents that are normally accessible only by the HR department or your administration. This can be very tempting, and requires you to develop the ability to refrain from accessing private areas without good reason. You may accidentally encounter confidential information when you are helping some-one in one of these departments resolve a computer issue; which requires you to develop an attitude of discretion.

You will need to decide how you will react if your administration or outside entities ask you to reveal information about your patrons' or your colleagues' usage of electronic resources, espe-cially if your institution does not have a specific policy protecting such information. You may also be confronted with other ethical issues. What will you do if you find out that a staff member has "borrowed" a library-purchased CD in order to install software on his home computer? If a member of your systems staff is using a large chunk of server storage for copyrighted MP3 files she has downloaded from the Internet? If you start a new position and find that the previous systems librarian at some point purchased a sin-gle copy of a software package and installed it on multiple machines? If a patron using a public-access Internet PC leaves a hacking or child pornography site prominently displayed on the monitor when he leaves the station?

You will encounter less clear-cut ethical challenges, as well. As a technological decision maker in a wired institution, you hold a great deal of power over people's computing environment. Avoid the temptation to allocate computing resources more heavily toward individuals you like or departments/functions you per-sonally prefer. Answer questions and resolve issues equally quickly; do not make this dependent on who is asking. A piece of advice often given to newer employees is to make friends with the janitor and the secretary, who each wield a great deal of power over your ability to work effectively—this extends also to "the systems person." Foster good relations with your coworkers, but never at the expense of others' needs.

These are issues for both libraries and individual systems librarians to grapple with. You will need to balance the good of your institution, the legality of users' actions, privacy considerations, and your personal ethical outlook in making tough decisions. Realize that, as in other areas of systems librarianship, there are often no simple answers, but you can draw on your library background to provide an ethical foundation for your technological outlook.

Works Cited

1. Manley, Will. "The Golden Rule of Supervision." *American Libraries*, February 2002: 88.

2. Tennant, Roy. "The Digital Librarian Shortage." *Library Journal*, March 15, 2002: 32.

3. "IT Salary Gender Gap?" *Information Week*, February 25, 2002: 75.

4. Sweat, Jeff. "Staying Put." *Information Week*, January 21, 2002: 36.

5. Kolb, Deborah M. and Ann C. Schaffner. "Negotiating What You're Worth." *Library Journal*, October 15, 2001: 53.

6. Godin, Seth. *Survival Is Not Enough: Zooming, Evolution, and the Future of Your Company.* New York City: The Free Press, 2002: 30.

7. Clark, Katie and Sally Kalin. "Technostressed Out?" *Library Journal*, August 1996: 31.

Conclusion

"Most of us view change as a threat, and survival as the goal. Change is not a threat, it's an opportunity, and survival is not the goal, transformative success is. It's thrilling if you give it a chance."
—Seth Godin[1]

Systems work in libraries presents a unique mix of frustrations, challenges, and triumphs. One guarantee: you'll never be bored. When deciding if systems is the path for you—or if you want to remain in your current career—assess your love for librarianship, technology, and change. Most people bitten by the technology bug never recover and go on to do some form of systems work throughout their career. Some do, however, choose to work in more traditional fields of librarianship for a time, and there is no shame in feeling burnt out!

While a number of respondents to the systems librarianship survey expressed some frustrations with their position, most were enthusiastic about their job, systems librarianship as a whole, and the future of the specialty. Most respondents emphasized the importance of thriving on constant technological change. Typical comments included:

- "You will never get bored. If you like change, living on the edge (at least the edge of the library), then this is the job for you."

- "I think I've chosen a very interesting and rewarding career. If more people knew how cool the job is, more aspiring librarians would go into systems. It's not an easy job—but it has a lot of fun challenges."

- "It has been, and continues to be, very rewarding. There's always a challenge, we're always busy, and we are at the forefront of change. It is nowhere to be for the faint of heart or the timid, which is one reason I like it so much!"

- "Being a Systems Librarian is most satisfying. It is challenging but I find that people in this field, which consists of computer experts and librarians, are natural teachers and love to share their expertise. It is a relatively new field and is changing constantly. This evolution provides opportunities for professional and personal growth."

- "The constant change that drives most librarians nuts keeps me from getting bored. I love having a new resource to learn or finding a new way to do something cheaper, faster, or better than before. If it weren't for the constant change, I'd probably do something else. Just maintaining existing systems is way too dull."

- "Systems work currently is one of the most exciting areas of librarianship, with numerous opportunities for those who are creative, dynamic, and personable. This subfield of librarianship is growing and changing. Keeping up requires one to be very proactive. Something new and different all the time has made coming to work enjoyable for me."

Many respondents mentioned that they had come to systems work from previous positions in specialties such as reference and cataloging. For many, systems work became the reason they stayed in the library field—after having found answering the same types of reference questions, for example, dull after several years, working with technology provided a fresh set of challenges and the opportunity to try something new. As Anne Beaumont, application support manager at the State Library of Victoria, explains: "It has never been boring in the last 10 years! I was bored at the repetitive nature of reference work after five years; in IT there is always something new happening."

Working with technology in libraries provides the opportunity to be on the forefront of change, and your responsibility for implementing new technologies and solutions should translate into a deserved sense of pride when you see those technologies used successfully by patrons and staff. Systems work allows librarians to feel a sense of accomplishment and to point to the often quite concrete results of their labors. This is especially true for those involved in large-scale projects and planning, who then have a finished product or service for which they deserve much of the credit. As Thomas Wilson writes: "A great deal of pride and ownership comes with these projects. When the library is thanked for providing services, the systems librarian can know that he or she made it happen."[2]

Pride, accomplishment, and the excitement of dealing with changing technology are just a few of the rewards inherent in an exciting and dynamic field of librarianship. Systems work, although it may undergo its own unforeseen transformations in a changing library future, promises to continue providing such rewards to those who stay the course.

Works Cited

1. Godin, Seth. *Survival Is Not Enough: Zooming, Evolution, and the Future of Your Company.* New York: Free Press, 2002: 4.

2. Wilson, Thomas C. *The Systems Librarian: Designing Roles, Defining Skills.* Chicago: ALA Editions, 1998: 176.

Appendix A

Accidental Systems Librarian Survey

This survey was posted as an online form at the library careers site http://www.lisjobs.com from late 2001 through early 2002. Announcements were posted on appropriate e-mail lists (SYSLIB-L, LIBNT-L, oss4lib, and Web4Lib) and the survey was also advertised on the front page of the Lisjobs.com Web site for job-seeking librarians.

Respondents are self-described systems librarians. This is not a scientific survey, and no attempt was made to qualify respondents as systems personnel prior to their answering these questions.

Accidental Systems Librarian Survey

Thanks for taking the time to complete this short survey about your career as a systems librarian. Your insights will help others who have found themselves on the same path! By filling out this survey, you are giving your permission to be quoted in a forthcoming book from Information Today. (If you would like to remain anonymous, please note that in your answers. Identifying details about your institution will be deleted from any quoted answers as well.)

Your Name:

Your E-mail Address:

Your Employer:

Your Job Title:

Would you like your answers to remain anonymous? (Y/N)

Do you have a library degree? If so, what year did you graduate?

Do you have additional degrees or certifications? If so, please specify.

What library positions have you held prior to your current job (if any)?

What technical positions have you held prior to your current job (if any)?

Please describe the path you took to systems librarianship.

Approximately what percentage of your time is devoted to "systems" responsibilities, including automation support, help desk, computer training, troubleshooting, Web development, etc.?

What do you most wish you'd learned in library school, that you instead have had to learn "on the job"?

What did you learn in library school that has proven especially useful on the job?

How do you use your skills as a librarian to perform systems duties effectively? (Provide examples if any spring to mind.)

What one piece of advice would you give to an aspiring library automation specialist?

What is your favorite tech support resource?

What is your favorite part of systems work?

What is the most frustrating part of systems work?

What type of formal training, if any, have you attended to help you keep up with new technological developments?

What other resources do you use to help keep yourself up-to-date?

Do you have any additional comments about your experiences with systems work in libraries?

Appendix B

Recommended Reading

Additional resources can be found interspersed throughout the chapters. These recommendations will supply useful background material as you prepare for your career in systems librarianship.

Chapter 1

Balas, Janet L. "Does Technology Define Librarians' Roles?" *Computers in Libraries*, November/December 2001: 58–60.

Beck, Maureen A. "Technology Competencies in the Continuous Quality Improvement Environment: A Framework for Appraising the Performance of Library Public Services Staff." *Library Administration & Management*, Spring 2002: 69–72.

Burke, John J. *Neal-Schuman Library Technology Companion: A Basic Guide for Library Staff.* New York: Neal-Schuman, 2001.

Donohue, Mary. "The Autobiography of a Modern Community College Librarian." *Computers in Libraries*, November/December 2001: 44–46.

Gordon, Rachel Singer. "A Course in Accidental Systems Librarianship." *Computers in Libraries*, November/December 2001: 24–28.

Gorman, Michael. "Human Values in a Technological Age." *Information Technology and Libraries* 20:1 (2001). 30 April 2002 (http://www.lita.org/ital/2001_gorman.html).

Latham, Joyce. "The World Online: IT Skills for the Practical Professional." *American Libraries*, March 2000: 40–42.

Lavagnino, Merri Beth. "Networking and the Role of the Academic Systems Librarian: An Evolutionary Perspective." *College & Research Libraries* 58(3): 217–231.

Marmion, Dan. "Facing the Challenge: Technology Training In Libraries." *Information Technology and Libraries* 17:4 (1998): 216.

Morgan, Eric Lease. "Computer Literacy for Librarians." *Computers in Libraries*, January 1998: 39–40.

Morgan, Eric Lease. "Systems Administration Requires People Skills." *Computers in Libraries*, March 1999: 36.

Saunders, Laverna M., ed. *The Evolving Virtual Library II: Practical and Philosophical Perspectives*. Medford, NJ: Information Today, Inc., 1999.

Schwartz, Mark. "Librarians and Technology: An Interview with Julie Bozzell." February 15, 2002. 1 May, 2002 (http://www.llrx.com/features/bozzell.htm).

Syracuse University School of Information Studies. "Librarians in the 21st Century: MIS in Libraries." Spring 2000. 24 February 2002 (http://istweb.syr.edu/21stcenlib/where/mis.html).

Tennant, Roy. "Honoring Technical Staff." *Library Journal*, May 15 2001. 4 May 2002 (http://libraryjournal.reviewsnews.com/index.asp?layout=articleArchive&articleId=CA75217).

Wilson, Thomas C. *The Systems Librarian: Designing Roles, Defining Skills*. Chicago: ALA Editions, 1998.

Chapter 2

Barclay, Donald A. *Managing Public-Access Computers: A How-To-Do-It Manual for Librarians*. New York: Neal-Schuman, 2000.

Benson, Allen C. "Building a Secure Library System." *Computers in Libraries*, March 1998. 2 March 2002 (http://www.infotoday.com/cilmag/mar98/story2.htm).

Benson, Allen C. *Securing PCs and Data in Libraries and Schools.* New York: Neal-Schuman, 1998.

Breeding, Marshall. "Defending Your Library Network." *Information Today,* September 2001: 46–47.

Breeding, Marshall. "Offering Remote Access to Restricted Resources." *Information Today,* May 2001: 52–53.

Chudnov, Daniel. "Open Source Software: The Future of Library Systems?" *Library Journal,* August 1999: 40–43.

Computers in Libraries, April 2002. (Thematic issue; digitizing content and making it Web-accessible.)

Crawford, Walt. "Talking 'Bout My Library." *American Libraries,* April 2002. 20 April 2002 (http://www.ala.org/alonline/crawford/cf402.html).

Howden, Norman. *Buying and Maintaining Personal Computers: A How-To-Do-It Manual for Librarians.* New York: Neal-Schuman, 2000.

Hunter, Gregory S. *Preserving Digital Information: A How-To-Do-It Manual for Librarians.* New York: Neal-Schuman, 2000.

Institute of Museum and Library Services. "Status of Technology and Digitization in the Nation's Museums and Libraries 2002 Report." May 10 2002. 8 June 2002 (http://www.imls.gov/Reports/TechReports/intro02.htm).

Jantz, Ronald. "E-Books and New Library Service Models: An Analysis of the Impact of E-Book Technology on Academic Libraries." *Information Technology and Libraries,* 20(2) 2001. April 15, 2002 (http://www.lita.org/ital/2002_jantz.html).

Mickey, Bill. "Open Source and Libraries: An Interview with Dan Chudnov." *Online,* January 2001. 9 May 2002 (http://www.infotoday.com/online/OL2001/mickey1_01.html).

Pfohl, Dan and Sherman Hayes. "Today's Systems Librarians Have a Lot to Juggle." *Computers in Libraries,* November/December 2001: 30–33.

Poynder, Richard. "The Open Source Movement." *Information Today*, October 2001: 1, 67, 69.

Randolph, Susan E. "Are E-Books In Your Future?" *Information Outlook*, February 2001: 22.

Saffady, William. *Introduction to Automation for Librarians, 4th ed.* Chicago: ALA Editions, 1999.

Chapter 3

Gregory, Vicki L. *Selecting and Managing Electronic Resources: A How-To-Do-It Manual for Librarians.* New York: Neal-Schuman, 2000.

Knight, Lorrie A. and Kimberly A. Lyons-Mitchell. "Measure For Measure: Statistics About Statistics." *Information Technology and Libraries*, 20(1) 2001: 34–38.

Schuyler, Michael. "Cutting-Edge Statistics." *Computers in Libraries*, March 2001: 51–53.

Chapter 4

Balas, Janet L. "Systems Administration: How to Avoid Reinventing the Wheel." *Computers in Libraries*, October 2000: 64.

Ballard, Terry. "Zen in the Art of Troubleshooting." *American Libraries*, January 1994: 108–110.

Bates, Mary Ellen. "The Newly Minted MLS: What Do We Need To Know Today?" *Searcher*, May 1998. 30 April 2002 (http://www.infotoday.com/searcher/may98/story1.htm).

Block, Carson. "In Search of System Stability." *netConnect* supplement to *Library Journal*, Winter 2001: 22–25.

Block, Marylaine. "Mapping the Information Landscape." *Searcher*, April 2002. 1 April 2002 (http://www.infotoday.com/searcher/apr02/block.htm).

McDermott, Irene E. "Digital Grease Monkeys: Librarians Who Dare to Repair." *Searcher*, October 2000: 10–14.

Chapter 5

Brandt, D. Scott. "E-mail Makes the World Go 'Round." *Computers in Libraries*, November/December 2000. 10 May 2002 (http://www.infotoday.com/cilmag/nov00/brandt.htm).

Brandt, D. Scott. "Technologists and Tinkerers." *Computers in Libraries*, November/December 2001: 55–57.

Crawford, Walt. "Talking About Public Access: PACS-L's First Decade." *Information Technology and Libraries*, 19(3) 2000. May 1, 2002 (http://www.lita.org/ital/1903_editorial.html).

Heiberger, Mary Morris and Julia Miller Vick. "Networking for Dummies." *The Chronicle of Higher Education*, May 17 2002. 19 May 2002 (http://chronicle.com/jobs/2002/05/2002051701c.htm).

Nesbeitt, Sarah L. and Rachel Singer Gordon. *The Information Professional's Guide to Career Development Online*. Medford, NJ: Information Today, 2002.

Ross, John B. and Don L. Bosseau. "Defining the Divide: Causes of Friction Between Librarians and Computer Support Staff." *Journal of Academic Librarianship*, 23(2) 1997: 132–133.

Xu, Hong. "Global Access and its Implications: The Use of Mailing Lists by Systems Librarians." *Proceedings of the American Society for Information Science Annual Meeting: Information Access in the Global Information Economy*. Pittsburgh, PA. October 25–29, 1998: 501–515.

Chapter 6

Akins, M. L. and J. R. Griffin. "Keys To Successful Systems Administration." *Computers in Libraries*, March 1999: 66.

Eastmond, Gwendolyn. "Technical Training: From 'Eeek!' to 'Oooh!'" *Library Administration & Management*, Spring 2002: 73–78.

Gordon, Rachel Singer. *Teaching the Internet in Libraries.* Chicago: ALA Editions, 2001.

Hollands, William D. *Teaching the Internet to Library Staff and Users: 10 Ready-To-Go Workshops That Work.* New York: Neal-Schuman, 1999.

Krissoff, Alan and Lee Konrad. "Computer Training for Staff and Patrons: A Comprehensive Academic Model." *Computers in Libraries*, January 1998. 28 May 2002 (http://www.infotoday. com/cilmag/jan98/story2.htm).

Massis, Bruce E. "How to Create and Implement a Technology Training Program." *American Libraries*, October 2001: 49–51.

McDermott, Irene E. "Solitaire Confinement: The Impact of the Physical Environment on Computer Training." *Computers in Libraries*, January 1998. 28 May 2002 (http://www.infotoday. com/cilmag/jan98/story1.htm).

Noble, Cherrie. "Reflecting On Our Future." *Computers in Libraries*, February 1998. 1 May 2002 (http://www.infotoday. com/cilmag/feb98/story2.htm).

Schneider, Karen. "The Old Guard and the New Technology." *Library Journal*, March 1, 1994: 64.

Tovell, Chris. "Whippersnappers vs. the Old Guard? Making E-Resources Training a Collaborative Experience." *Info Career Trends*, September 2001. 4 January 2002 (http://www.lisjobs. com/newsletter/archives/sept01ctovell.htm).

Weiss, Elaine. *The Accidental Trainer: You Know Computers, So They Want You To Teach Everyone Else.* Jossey-Bass, 1996.

Webster, Monica R. "Let Your Fingers Do the Training." *Library Software Review*, 18(1/2) 1999: 4–12.

Chapter 7

Clark, Sue. "IT Training Rip-Offs." *Network World*, March 25, 2002: 44–48.

Cohen, Steven. "RSS For Non-Techie Librarians." *LLRX.com*, June 3 2002. 10 June 2002. (http://www.llrx.com/features/rssforlibrarians. htm).

O'Leary, Mick. "New Roles Come of Age." *Online*, March 2000: 20–22, 24–25.

Chapter 8

Breeding, Marshall. "Capturing the Migrating Customer." *Library Journal*, April 1, 2002: 48–60.

Breeding, Marshall. "The Open Source ILS: Still Only a Distant Possibility." *Information Technology and Libraries*, 21(1) 2002: 16–18.

Cohn, John M., Ann L. Kelsey and Keith Michael Fields. *Planning for Integrated Library Systems and Technologies.* New York: Neal-Schuman, 2001.

Doering, William. "Managing the Transition to a New Library Catalog: Tips for Smooth Sailing." *Computers in Libraries*, July/August 2000. 29 April 2002 (http://www.infotoday.com/ cilmag/jul00/doering.htm).

Martin, Mary C. "Managing Your Library's Computer Nerds." *Computers in Libraries*, February 1999: 8.

Mayo, Diane and Sandra Nelson. *Wired for the Future: Developing Your Library Technology Plan.* Chicago: ALA Editions, 1999.

McCarthy, Meredith. "Project URL: A Helping Hand for Choosing a Library Information System." May 1999. 23 February 2002. (http://www.coe.missouri.edu/~is334/projects/Project_URL/ implementation.html).

Ralston, Rick, Margaret A. Rioux, and Kathryn D. Ellis. "With Feet Planted Firmly In Mid-Air: Staff Training For Automation System Migration." *The Serials Librarian*, 36(3/4) 1999: 407–413.

Tebbetts, Diane R. "The Costs of Information Technology and the Electronic Library." *The Electronic Library*, 18(2) 2000: 127–136.

Tennant, Roy. "The Most Important Management Decision: Hiring Staff for the New Millennium." *Library Journal*, February 15 1998. 4 May 2002 (http://libraryjournal.reviewsnews.com/index.asp?layout=articleArchive&articleId=CA156490).

Youngman, Daryl C. "Library Staffing Considerations in the Age of Technology." *Issues in Science and Technology Librarianship* Fall 1999. 6 June 2002 (http://www.library.ucsb.edu/istl/99-fall/article5.html).

Chapter 9

Clark, Katie and Sally Kalin. "Technostressed Out?" *Library Journal*, August 1996: 30–32.

Jones, Dorothy E. "Ten Years Later: Support Staff Perceptions and Opinions on Technology in the Workplace." *Library Trends*, 47(4) 1999: 711–741.

Kolb, Deborah M. and Ann C. Schaffner. "Negotiating What You're Worth." *Library Journal*, October 15, 2001: 52–53.

Kupersmith, John. "John Kupersmith's Technostress Page." 19 May 2002 (http://www.jkup.net/tstress.html).

Moore, Katherine L. Bell and Karen C. Knox. "How Can We Survive In Reality Library?" *Computers in Libraries*, November/December 2001: 34–38.

Saunders, Laverna. "Systems Administrators: The Unsung Library Heroes." *Computers in Libraries*, March 1999: 47.

Schulman, Sandy. "Applying a Proactive Ounce of Prevention." *Information Today*, July/August 1998: 46.

Stover, Mark. *Leading the Wired Organization: The Information Professional's Guide to Managing Technological Change.* New York: Neal-Schuman, 1999.

Sweat, Jeff. "Staying Put." *InformationWeek*, January 21, 2002: 36–42.

Tennant, Roy. "The Digital Librarian Shortage." *Library Journal*, 15 March 2002: 32.

Thompson, Susan. "Riding Into Uncharted Territory: The New Systems Librarian." *Computers in Libraries*, March 1999: 14–18.

Weissman, Sara. "Shoptalk Answers To Real-World Problems." *netConnect* supplement to *Library Journal*, October 15, 1999: 20.

Xu, Hong and Hsin-liang Chen. "What Do Employers Expect? The Educating Systems Librarians Research Project Report 1." *The Electronic Library*, 17(3) 1999: 171–179.

Xu, Hong and Hsin-liang Chen. "Whom Do Employers Actually Hire? The Educating Systems Librarians Research Project Report 2." *The Electronic Library*, 18(3) 2000: 171–182.

Conclusion

Godin, Seth. *Survival Is Not Enough: Zooming, Evolution, and the Future of Your Company.* New York: Free Press, 2002.

Appendix C

Web Sites
http://www.lisjobs.com/tasl/

Chapter 1

Photohistory of Computing and Libraries
http://valinor.ca/computing

Franklin Park Library
http://www.franklinparklibrary.org

Oakland Public Library Staff Technology Competencies
http://www.oaklandlibrary.org/techcomp.htm

New Jersey Library Association Technical Competencies
http://www.njla.org/statements/techcompetencies.html

Rochester Regional Library Council Core Competencies
http://www.rrlc.org/competencies/techcomp.html

Library of Congress, Knowledge, Skills and Abilities for Systems
Librarians
http://www.loc.gov/flicc/wg/ksa-sys.html

Chapter 2

kbAlertz
http://www.kbalertz.com

Microsoft Security Portal
http://www.microsoft.com/security

Andrew Mutch's IE Configuration Pages
http://tln.lib.mi.us/~amutch/pro/ie

Public Web Browser
http://teamsoftware.bizland.com/projects.htm

Microsoft Support
http://support.microsoft.com

Woody's Watch
http://www.woodyswatch.com

Windows Annoyances
http://www.annoyances.org

Apple Support
http://www.apple.com/support

MacFixIt
http://www.macfixit.com

Macworld
http://www.macworld.com

TidBITS
http://www.tidbits.com

General Public License
http://www.gnu.org/copyleft/gpl.html

OSS4lib
http://www.oss4lib.org

OSS4lib e-mail list
http://www.oss4lib.org/listserv

OSSNLibraries
http://dewey.library.nd.edu/ossnlibraries/portal

OSSNLibraries—Open Source Software LN Libraries
http://www.infomotions.com/musings/ossnlibraries.shtml

Linux In the Library
http://gromit.westminster.lib.co.us/linux/linux-library.html

Information Technology and Libraries, March 2002
http://www.lita.org/ital/ital2101.html

Wireless Librarian
http://people.morrisville.edu/~drewwe/wireless

Wireless LANS
http://www.pla.org/publications/technotes/technotes_lans.html

Look Ma, No Wires!
http://www.infotoday.com/cilmag/mar01/glover.htm

The Handheld Librarian Weblog
http://www.handheldlib.blogspot.com

Innovative Interfaces' AirPAC
http://www.iii.com/pdf/airpac.pdf

EZProxy
http://www.usefulutilities.com/ezproxy

Epixtech's Remote Patron Authentication
http://www.epixtech.com/products/rpa.asp

Library Web Manager's Reference Center
http://sunsite.berkeley.edu/Web4Lib/RefCenter

A List Apart
http://alistapart.com

Metronet's Links for Library Webmasters
http://www.metronet.lib.mn.us/libpage/links.cfm

Innovative Internet Applications in Libraries
http://www.wiltonlibrary.org/innovate.html

PLA TechNote on Intranets
http://www.pla.org/publications/technotes/technotes_
intranet.html

Ad-Aware
http://www.lsfileserv.com

FoolProof Security
http://www.smartstuff.com/fps/fpsmac.html

RLG DigiNews
http://www.rlg.org/preserv/diginews

Digital Reference Services Bibliography
http://www.lis.uiuc.edu/~b-sloan/digiref.html

OCLC's SiteSearch
https://www.sitesearch.oclc.org

WebFeat
http://www.webfeat.org

Serials Solutions
http://www.serialssolutions.com

Chapter 3

Library Statistics and Measures
http://web.syr.edu/%7Ejryan/infopro/stats.html

Analog
http://www.analog.cx

Sawmill
http://www.sawmill.net

Searchtools.com
http://www.searchtools.com

SnagIt
http://www.techsmith.com

Chapter 4

CNET
http://www.cnet.com

LIBNT-L
http://listserv.utk.edu/archives/libnt-l.html

Microsoft Support
http://support.microsoft.com

Microsoft TechNet
http://www.microsoft.com/technet

O'Reilly & Associates
http://www.ora.com

SYSLIB-L
http://listserv.acsu.buffalo.edu/archives/syslib-l.html

TechRepublic.com
http://www.techrepublic.com

Web4Lib
http://sunsite.berkeley.edu/Web4Lib

ZDNet
http://www.zdnet.com

LITA Publications
http://www.lita.org/litapubs

FreeAnswers
http://www.freeanswers.com

Free Trial Zone
http://freetrialzone.com

Chapter 5

DIG_REF
http://www.vrd.org/Dig_Ref/dig_ref.shtml

DIGLIB
http://www.ifla.org/II/lists/diglib.htm

Electronic Resources In Libraries
http://www.topica.com/lists/eril

LIBNT-L
http://listserv.utk.edu/archives/libnt-l.html

Libsoft
http://www.orst.edu/groups/libsoft

Linux-in-libraries
http://apocalypse.unomaha.edu/lil

LITA-L
http://www.lita.org/lists.htm

NETTRAIN
http://listserv.acsu.buffalo.edu/archives/nettrain.html

oss4lib-discuss
http://lists.sourceforge.net/lists/listinfo/oss4lib-discuss

oss4lib
http://www.oss4lib.org

PACS-L
http://info.lib.uh.edu/pacsl.html

Perl4Lib
http://www.rice.edu/perl4lib

Public Library Computer Trainers
http://www.topica.com/lists/publibct

Syslib-L
http://listserv.acsu.buffalo.edu/archives/syslib-l.html

Web4Lib
http://sunsite.berkeley.edu/Web4Lib

XML4Lib
http://sunsite.berkeley.edu/XML4Lib/

Library-Oriented Lists
http://liblists.wrlc.org/home.htm

Topica
http://www.topica.com

PAML
http://paml.net

CataList
http://www.lsoft.com/catalist.html

SysAds.org
http://www.sysads.org

ILA RSTF Technology Users Group Blog
http://www.techusers.blogspot.com

ASIS&T 2001 Annual Conference Page
http://www.asis.org/digiscript.html

LITA Regional Institutes
http://www.lita.org/institut

Chapter 6

LanSchool
http://www.lanschool.com

Net-Support School
http://www.netsupport-inc.com

SnagIt
http://www.techsmith.com

Macromedia Dreamweaver CourseBuilder Extension
http://www.macromedia.com/software/coursebuilder

PowerPoint 2002 Producer Add-In
http://office.microsoft.com/downloads/2002/producer.
aspx

Techsmith's Camtasia
http://www.techsmith.com/products/camtasia/camtasia.asp

Testcraft Standard Edition
http://www.testcraft.com/FeaSTD.asp

TILT
http://tilt.lib.utsystem.edu

Washoe County Library System Mouse Tutorial
http://www.washoe.lib.nv.us/pub_mouse.html

Chapter 7

Barnes & Noble University
http://www.barnesandnobleuniversity.com

FindTutorials.com
http://www.findtutorials.com

Learn2
http://www.tutorials.com

Learnthat.com
http://www.learnthat.com/courses/computer

OCLC Institute
http://institute.oclc.org

TechTutorials
http://www.techtutorials.com

Trainingtools.com
http://trainingtools.com

W3Schools
http://www.w3schools.com

ARL Online Lyceum
http://www.arl.org/arl/workshops.html

NSLS Continuing Education Workshops
http://www.nslsilus.org/ce

UW Madison SLIS Continuing Education
http://www.slis.wisc.edu/academic/ces

UM SI Digital Tool Kits
http://www.si.umich.edu/dtk

Library Techlog
http://www.meberle.com/weblog.html

LISNews.com
http://www.lisnews.com

SAPL Extra net
http://extra.sapl.ab.ca

The Shifted Librarian
http://www.theshiftedlibrarian.com

SysAds.org
http://www.sysads.org

Radio UserLand
http://radio.userland.com

AmphetaDesk
http://www.disobey.com/amphetadesk

InfoToday NewsBreaks
http://www.infotoday.com/newsbreaks/breaks.htm

InfoWorld
http://www.iwsubscribe.com/newsletters

LangaList
http://www.langa.com/newsletter.htm

Lockergnome
http://www.lockergnome.com

NetworkWorld
http://www.nwwsubscribe.com/news

Woody's Watch
http://www.wopr.com

Government Technology
http://www.govtech.net

Presentations Magazine
http://www.presentations.com

LITA's Tech Experts' Reading Habits
http://www.lita.org/committe/toptech/expertsread.htm

Technology Electronic Reviews
http://www.lita.org/ter

Technology Grant News
http://www.technologygrantnews.com

Chapter 8

Technology Planning
http://web.syr.edu/~jryan/infopro/techplan.html

ILS Reports
http://www.ilsr.com/tech.htm

Sample RFPs
http://www.ilsr.com/sample.htm

Avanti
http://www.nslsilus.org/~schlumpf/avanti

Koha
http://www.koha.org

LearningAccess ILS
http://www.learningaccess.org/website/techdev/ils.php

OpenOPAC
http://openopac.sourceforge.net

Open Source Digital Library System Project
http://osdls.library.arizona.edu

PHP MyLibrary
http://phpmylibrary.sourceforge.net

Escape From the Library Mansion
http://www.slco.lib.ut.us/library_mansion

Closing In On Content
http://libraryjournal.reviewnews.com/index.asp?layout=
articleArchive&articleId=CA74708

Managing the Transition to a New Library Catalog
http://www.infotoday.com/cilmag/jul00/doering.htm

ILS Reports
http://www.ilsr.com

Library Automation Consultants
http://www.libraryhq.com/consultants.html

Chapter 9

LITA Online Jobline
http://www.lita.org/jobs

ASIST Online Jobline
http://www.asis.org/Jobline

Lisjobs.com
http://www.lisjobs.com

Library Job Postings On the Internet
http://www.libraryjobpostings.org

Information Today Journals
http://www.infotoday.com/periodicals.htm

Technology Electronic Reviews
http://www.lita.org/ter

Free Pint
http://www.freepint.co.uk

About the Author

Rachel Singer Gordon is the former Head of Computer Services at the Franklin Park (Illinois) Public Library. She is the founder and Webmaster of the library career site Lisjobs.com, from which she also publishes *Info Career Trends*, a free, bimonthly electronic newsletter on career development issues for librarians. Since 2001, she has been the "Computer Media" review columnist for *Library Journal.* She has written and presented widely on the intersections between technology and librarianship, and her published work includes *Teaching the Internet in Libraries* (ALA Editions, 2001) and *The Information Professional's Guide to Career Development Online* (with Sarah Nesbeitt, Information Today, Inc., 2002). Rachel holds an MLIS from Dominican University and an MA from Northwestern University.

Index

More Great Books from Information Today, Inc.

The Accidental Webmaster

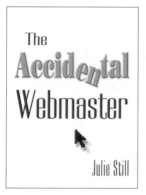

By Julie Still

Here is a lifeline for the individual who has not been trained as a Webmaster, but who—whether by choice or under duress—has become one nonetheless. While most Webmastering books focus on programming and related technical issues, *The Accidental Webmaster* helps readers deal with the full range of challenges they face on the job. Author, librarian, and accidental Webmaster Julie Still offers advice on getting started, setting policies, working with ISPs, designing home pages, selecting content, drawing site traffic, gaining user feedback, fundraising, avoiding copyright problems, and much more.

2003/softbound/ISBN 1-57387-164-8 $29.50

The Information Professional's Guide to Career Development Online

By Rachel Singer Gordon and Sarah L. Nesbeitt

This book is designed to meet the needs of librarians interested in using online tools to advance their careers. It offers practical advice on topics ranging from current awareness services and personal Web pages to distance education, electronic resumes, and online job searches. New librarians will learn how to use the Internet to research education opportunities, and experienced info pros will learn ways to network through online conferences and discussion lists. Supported by a Web page.

2002/softbound/ISBN 1-57387-124-9 $29.50

The Librarian's Internet Survival Guide

Strategies for the High-Tech Reference Desk

By Irene E. McDermott
Edited by Barbara Quint

In this authoritative and tremendously useful guide, Irene McDermott helps her fellow reference librarians succeed in the bold new world of the Web. *The Survival Guide* provides easy access to the information librarians need when the pressure is on: trouble-shooting tips and advice, Web resources for answering reference questions, and strategies for managing information and keeping current. In addition to helping librarians make the most of Web tools and resources, McDermott covers a full range of important issues including Internet training, privacy, child safety, helping patrons with special needs, building library Web pages, and much more.

2002/296 pp/softbound/ISBN 1-57387-129-X $29.50

The OPL Sourcebook

A Guide for Solo and Small Libraries

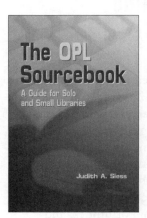

By Judith A. Siess

Judith A. Siess, editor of the monthly newsletter, "The One-Person Library," has created the definitive handbook and directory for small and one-person libraries (OPLs). Taking an international approach to reflect the growing number of OPLs worldwide, this new book covers organizational culture, customer service, time management and planning, budgeting, accounting, technology, collection development, education, downsizing, outsourcing, and many other key management issues. Includes a comprehensive directory.

2001/260 pp/hardbound/ISBN 1-57387-111-7 $39.50

Creating Web-Accessible Databases

Case Studies for Libraries, Museums, and Other Nonprofits

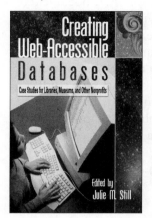

Edited by Julie M. Still

Libraries, museums, and other not-for-profit institutions are increasingly looking for (and finding) ways to offer patrons and the public Web access to their collections. This book from Julie Still and her expert contributors explores the unique challenges nonprofit archival institutions face in leveraging the Internet and presents a dozen case studies showcasing a variety of successful projects and approaches.

2001/200 pp/hardbound/ISBN 1-57387-104-4 $39.50

Directory of Library Automation Software, Systems, and Services

2002–2003 Ed.

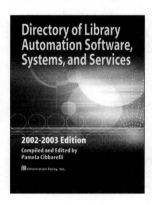

Edited by Pamela Cibarelli

Published biennially since 1983, the *Directory of Library Automation Software, Systems, and Services* is recognized as the primary reference source for software packages used in automating libraries. This entirely new and expanded edition includes information on software for library automation, information management, text retrieval, and citation management. Library automation tools, retrospective conversion products and services, Internet resources on the topic of library automation, database hosts, CD-ROM distributors, library automation books and serials, and over 100 important meetings and conferences are also covered.

2002/351 pp/softbound/ISBN 1-57387-140-0 $89.00

The Evolving Virtual Library II

Edited by Laverna M. Saunders

The Evolving Virtual Library II documents how libraries of all types are changing with the integration of the Internet and the Web, electronic resources, and computer networks. It provides a summary of trends, developments in networking, case studies of creating digital content delivery systems for remote users, applications in K-12 and public libraries, and a vision of things to come.

1999/194 pp/hardbound/ISBN 1-57387-070-6 $39.50

Library Relocations and Collection Shifts

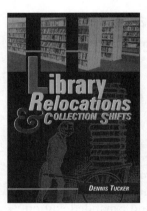

By Dennis C. Tucker

In *Library Relocations and Collection Shifts*, author, librarian, and move director Dennis C. Tucker explains how to develop an appropriate moving plan for a library of any type or size. A thorough revision of his classic, *From Here to There: Moving a Library*, the book provides coverage of all these topics and more:

• Appointing a moving director and committee
• Moving methods and strategies
• Customizing a moving plan for your library
• Planning and coordinating the move
• Handling books and periodicals
• Cleaning, fumigation, and deacidfication
• Working with professional movers
• Communicating with staff and the public

1999/212 pp/hardbound/ISBN 1-57387-069-2 $35.00

Building and Running a Successful Research Business

A Guide for the Independent Information Professional

By Mary Ellen Bates
Edited by Reva Basch

This is *the* handbook every aspiring independent information professional needs to launch, manage, and build a research business. Organized into four sections, "Getting Started," "Running the Business," "Marketing," and "Researching," the book walks you through every step of the process. Author and independent researcher Mary Ellen Bates covers everything from "is this right for you?" to closing the sale, managing the clients, promoting your business on the Web, and tapping into powerful information sources beyond the Web.

2003/360 pp/softbound/ISBN 0-910965-62-5 $29.95

Super Searchers Make It on Their Own

Top Independent Information Professionals Share Their Secrets for Starting and Running a Research Business

By Suzanne Sabroski
Edited by Reva Basch

If you want to start and run a successful Information Age business, read this book. Here, for the first time anywhere, 11 of the world's top research entrepreneurs share their strategies for starting a business, developing a niche, finding clients, doing the research, networking with peers, and staying up-to-date with Web resources and technologies. You'll learn how these super searchers use the Internet to find, organize, analyze, and package information for their clients. Most importantly, you'll discover their secrets for building a profitable research business.

2002/336 pp/softbound/ISBN 0-910965-59-5 $24.95

The Invisible Web

Uncovering Information Sources
Search Engines Can't See

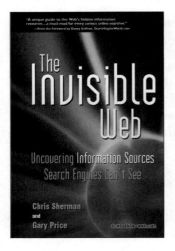

By Chris Sherman and Gary Price
Foreword by Danny Sullivan

Most of the authoritative information accessible over the Internet is invisible to search engines like AltaVista, HotBot, and Google. This invaluable material resides on the "Invisible Web," which is largely comprised of content-rich databases from universities, libraries, associations, businesses, and government agencies around the world.

Authors Chris Sherman and Gary Price—two of the world's leading Invisible Web experts—are on a mission to save you time and aggravation and help you succeed in your information quest. They introduce you to top sites and sources and offer tips, techniques, and analysis that will let you pull needles out of haystacks every time. Supported by a dynamic Web page.

CyberAge Books/402 pp/Softbound/ISBN 0-910965-51-X $29.95

The Extreme Searcher's Guide to Web Search Engines, 2nd Edition

A Handbook for the Serious Searcher

By Randolph Hock
Foreword by Reva Basch

In this completely revised and expanded version of his award-winning book, the "extreme searcher," Randolph (Ran) Hock, digs even deeper, covering all the most popular Web search tools, plus a half-dozen of the newest and most exciting search engines to come down the pike. This is a practical, user-friendly guide supported by a regularly updated Web site.

**2001/250 pp/softbound
ISBN 0-910965-47-1 $24.95**

Web of Deception

Misinformation on the Internet

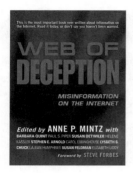

Edited by Anne P. Mintz
Foreword by Steve Forbes

"Experts here walk you through the risks and traps of the Web world and tell you how to avoid them or to fight back ... Anne Mintz and her collaborators have done us a genuine service." —Steve Forbes, from the Foreword

Intentionally misleading or erroneous information on the Web can wreak havoc on your health, privacy, investments, business decisions, online purchases, legal affairs, and more. Until now, the breadth and significance of this growing problem have yet to be fully explored. In *Web of Deception*, Anne P. Mintz brings together 10 information industry gurus to illuminate the issues and help you recognize and deal with the flood of deception and misinformation in a range of critical subject areas.

2002/278 pp/softbound/ISBN 0-910965-60-9 $24.95

Net Crimes & Misdemeanors

Outmaneuvering the Spammers, Swindlers, and Stalkers Who Are Targeting You Online

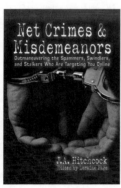

By J.A. Hitchcock
Edited by Loraine Page

Cyber crime expert J.A. Hitchcock helps individuals and business users of the Web protect themselves, their children, and their employees against online cheats and predators. Hitchcock details a broad range of abusive practices, shares victims' stories, and offers advice on how to handle junk e-mail, "flaming," privacy invasion, financial scams, cyberstalking, and indentity theft. She provides tips and techniques that can be put to immediate use and points to the laws, organizations, and Web resources that can aid victims and help them fight back. Supported by a Web site.

2002/384 pp/softbound/ISBN 0-910965-57-9 $24.95

Electronic Democracy, 2nd Edition

Using the Internet to Transform American Politics

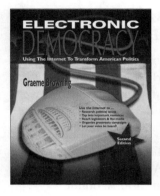

By Graeme Browning
Foreword by Adam Clayton Powell III

In this new edition of *Electronic Democracy*, award-winning journalist and author Graeme Browning details the colorful history of politics and the Net, describes key Web-based sources of political information, offers practical techniques for influencing legislation online, and provides a fascinating, realistic vision of the future.

2002/200 pp/softbound/ISBN 0-910965-49-8 $19.95

Naked in Cyberspace, 2nd Edition

How to Find Personal Information Online

By Carole A. Lane
Foreword by Beth Givens

In this fully revised and updated second edition of her bestselling guide, author Carole A. Lane surveys the types of personal records that are available on the Internet and online services. Lane explains how researchers find and use personal data, identifies the most useful sources of information about people, and offers advice for readers with privacy concerns. You'll learn how to use online tools and databases to gain competitive intelligence, locate and investigate people, access public records, identify experts, find new customers, recruit employees, search for assets, uncover criminal records, conduct genealogical research, and much more.

2002/586 pp/softbound/ISBN 0-910965-50-1 $29.95